£1.75
In UK only

SBN 361 04152 7

"Secret Seven Mystery" first published by Brockhampton Press (now Hodder and Stoughton Children's Books) in 1957
Published 1978 by Purnell Books, Berkshire House, Queen Street, Maidenhead, Berkshire
Made and printed in Great Britain by Purnell and Sons Limited, Paulton (Bristol) and London

Enid Blyton's

Secret Seven

Mystery Annual

Purnell

Contents

PETER

Peter is Janet's brother and the leader of the Secret Seven. The Seven meet in a shed in Peter and Janet's garden, and Peter makes sure they abide by the rules of the society, using the correct password and wearing their special badges. Peter is quick-witted and spirited, and is looked up to by the other members of the Seven.

JANET

Janet is Peter's sister, and together they invented the Secret Seven. Janet is at school with Pam and Barbara, and is the most resourceful and independent of the three girls. Unlike some brothers and sisters, she and Peter get on well, and work happily together in the Seven!

COLIN

Colin is a schoolfriend of Peter, George and Jack. He and George often work as a pair on the Secret Seven's adventures. He is quieter than Peter or Jack, and usually follows their instructions.

BARBARA

Barbara is at school with Janet and Pam. She is a sensible and reliable member of the Seven, but is a little more timid and cautious than the other two girls.

PAM

Pam is a schoolfriend of Janet and Barbara. She is quite adventurous, but can be a little quarrelsome and stubborn sometimes! Peter keeps her in line, though!

GEORGE

George is at school with Colin, Peter and Jack. He and Colin often work together on the Seven's tasks. He is a helpful member of the Seven, but not a natural leader.

JACK

Jack is brave and energetic and is really second in command of the Seven after Peter. He usually accompanies Peter on the more difficult and dangerous of the Secret Seven's adventures. He has a mischievous sister called Susie, who is not a member of the Seven, and who is always trying to ruin their plans!

Introduction

We're proud to present a brand new annual, based on the adventures of the Secret Seven —some of Enid Blyton's most famous and popular characters.

This annual is quite different from anything you've read before. First of all it contains the whole of one of the Seven's most exciting adventures—'Secret Seven Mystery'—partly as picture strip, partly as narrative, and fully illustrated in colour and black and white. The annual also contains all sorts of interesting features and activities, linked to the events in the title story. Animal lovers will find an article on horses at work and a feature on puppy care. If you like cooking there are some tasty recipes to try, and for enthusiastic cyclists there are tips on looking after your bike.

You'll find all this, together with other projects, quizzes and puzzles in these pages.

The *Secret Seven Annual* has a companion—the *Famous Five Annual*—so look out for that one too!

CHAPTER ONE

Something Interesting

PETER and Janet were having breakfast with their father and mother one lovely spring morning. Scamper, their golden spaniel, was lying as usual under the table.

'Dad,' began Peter, but his mother frowned at him.

'Your father is reading the paper,' she said. 'Don't bother him just now!'

His father put down the paper and smiled. 'Do the Secret Seven want to make themselves really useful?' he asked. 'Because I've just read something in my paper that may be right up their street!'

'Oh, Dad—what?' cried Peter, and Janet put down her egg-spoon and looked at him expectantly.

'It's about a girl who's run away from home,' said their father, looking at his paper. 'She stole some money from the desk of her form-mistress, but when the police went to see her aunt about it, she ran away.'

'But—what can the Secret Seven do about it?' asked Peter, surprised.

'Listen—I'll read you the piece,' said his father, and propped the paper up in front of him again. 'Elizabeth Mary Wilhemina Sonning, after being accused of stealing money from the desk of her form-mistress, was found to be missing from her aunt's home. She took nothing with her but the clothes she was wearing, and is in school uniform and school hat. It is stated that her parents are abroad, and that she has a brother who is at present away in France.'

Peter's father looked up from the paper. 'Now comes the bit that might interest *you*,' he said. 'Elizabeth was seen on the evening of that day in Belling Village, and it is thought that she might be going to her grandmother, who lives not far off.'

'Belling Village! Why that's the next village to ours,' said Janet. 'Oh—you think the Secret Seven could keep a look-out for Elizabeth, Daddy! Yes—we could! What's she like?'

'There's a photograph here,' said her father, and passed the paper across. 'Not a very good one—but in her school uniform, which is a help.'

Peter and Janet stared at the picture in the paper. They saw the photograph of a merry, laughing girl a little older than themselves, with a mass of fluffy hair round her face. They thought she looked rather nice.

Though she can't be really, if she stole money and then ran away, thought Janet. She turned to her father. 'Whereabouts in Belling Village does her granny live?'

'It doesn't say, does it?' said her father, reaching for his paper again. 'You'll have to read this evening's paper and see if there are any more details. If the child goes to her granny's she'll be

Janet sat down to write notices to each of the Secret Seven. Peter signed each one

found at once, of course. But if she hides somewhere around the place, you might be able to spot her.'

'Yes. We might,' said Peter. 'The Secret Seven haven't had *anything* interesting to do lately. We'll call a meeting tomorrow. Good thing it's Saturday!'

That evening, Janet sat down to write notices to each of the Secret Seven to call them to a meeting the next day. Each notice said the same things.

'Dear S.S. Member,

A meeting will be held tomorrow morning, Saturday, at ten sharp, in the shed. Wear your badge and remember the password.'

Peter signed each one, and then he and Janet fetched their bicycles and rode off to deliver the notices, Scamper trotting beside them. They felt pleasantly excited. This new affair might not come to anything—but at least it was something to talk about and to make plans for.

'We'd better buy an evening paper on our way back and see if there's anything else in it about Elizabeth Mary Wilhemina Sonning,' said Peter.

So they stopped at the little news-agent's shop and bought one. They stood outside the shop, eagerly looking through the pages for any mention of the runaway girl. At last they found a small paragraph, headed 'MISSING GIRL'.

'Here it is,' said Peter, thrilled. 'Look, Janet, it says, "Elizabeth Sonning is still missing, and her grandmother states that she has not seen her. Anyone seeing a child whose appearance tallies with the following description is asked to get in touch with the police." Then, see, Janet, there's a good description of her. That's fine—we can read it out to the Seven tomorrow.'

'Good!' said Janet. 'Come on, Scamper—we'll have to bike home pretty fast, so you'll have to run at top speed!'

Scamper puffed and panted after them, his long silky ears flopping up and down as he ran. He wasn't a member of the Secret Seven, but he certainly belonged! No meeting was complete without him.

'What's the password, Peter?' asked Janet, as they put their bicycles away. 'It's ages since we had a meeting.'

'It's a jolly good thing *I* never forget it,' said Peter. 'I shan't tell it to you—but I'll give you a hint. Think of *lamb*—that ought to remind you!'

'Lamb?' said Janet, puzzled. 'Well—it reminds me of sheep, Peter—or Mary had a little lamb—or lamb chops. Which is it?'

'None of them!' said Peter, grinning. 'Have another shot, Janet—and tell me at the meeting tomorrow!'

'Look, Janet, it says, "Elizabeth Sonning is still missing and her grandmother has not seen her"'

CHAPTER TWO

Knock-Knock

'HAVE you remembered the password yet?' asked Peter next morning, when Janet and he were tidying their shed ready for the meeting.

'No, I haven't,' said Janet. 'And I think you might tell me, because you know jolly well I've got to come. I've been thinking of lamb—lamb—lamb for ages, but it doesn't remind me of anything except what I've already told you. Tell me the word, Peter, do!'

'No,' said Peter firmly. 'You're always forgetting. It's time you were taught a lesson. I shan't let you into the meeting unless you remember it. Look—go and ask mummy if we can have some of those biscuits she made last week.'

'Go yourself,' said Janet, crossly.

'I'm the head of the Secret Seven,' said Peter. 'Obey orders, Janet!'

Janet went off, not feeling at all pleased. She was quite afraid that Peter *wouldn't* let her into the meeting! He was very strict about rules.

She went into the kitchen, but mummy wasn't there. Some lamb chops lay on the table, and Janet looked at them frowning. 'Lamb! Oh dear—whatever ought you to remind me of? I simply can't think! Oh—here's mummy. Mummy, *may* we have some of your ginger biscuits, please? Oh, what's that you've got? Mint—let me smell it. I love the smell. I wouldn't mind mint scent on my hanky!'

'It's for mint sauce with the chops,' said mummy. 'Now I'll just—'

'Mint sauce! Of *course*! That's the password, Mint sauce! What a fathead I am!' said Janet. Then she grew serious and looked solemnly at her mother.

'I shouldn't have said the password out loud! We're not supposed to tell a soul. Mummy, don't remember it, will you?'

'What are you gabbling about?' said her mother, and went to get her tin of ginger biscuits. 'Here you are—you can have all of these. I'm making some more for tomorrow.'

'Oh, *thank* you!' said Janet, delighted, and skipped off down the garden with the tin. As she came near the shed she shouted out to Peter.

'Mint sauce, mint sauce, mint sauce!'

'Have you gone mad?' said a cross voice, and Peter looked out of the shed, frowning. 'Shouting out the password for everyone to know! I'm glad you've remembered it at last.'

'Well, mummy came in with mint to make mint sauce. Wasn't it lucky?' said Janet. 'Oh, Scamper, you know I've got some ginger biscuits, don't you? I expect there'll be one for you. Peter, it's almost ten o'clock.'

'I know,' said Peter. 'I'm just ready. Are there enough things to sit on? You'll have to sit on that big flower-pot, Janet. The gardener must have taken away

'That's just what this meeting is about,' said Peter. 'Now listen!'

'Shut the door, Janet, please'

our seventh box.'

Scamper began to bark. 'That's someone coming already,' said Peter. 'Shut the door, Janet, please. We'll have to ask the password as usual.'

Knock—knock!

'Password!' called Peter.

'Mint sauce!' said two voices.

'Enter!' said Peter, and Janet opened the door. 'Hello, George and Colin. You're jolly punctual.'

Knock—knock!

'Password!' shouted Peter. A cautious voice came in through the keyhole.

'I've forgotten. But I'm Pam, so you can let me in.'

'No, we can't. You know the rule,' said Peter, sternly.

'Think of lamb chops!' called Janet, before Peter could stop her.

A giggle was heard. 'Oh, yes—of course, MINT SAUCE.'

Janet opened the door, but Peter looked quite cross. 'How dare you remind Pam like that?' he demanded.

'Well, *you* reminded me!' said Janet, indignantly. 'You said, "think of lamb chops", didn't you?'

'There's someone else coming,' said Peter, changing the subject hurriedly.

Knock—knock! 'Mint sauce,' said two voices.

'Come in!' shouted Peter, and in came Jack and Barbara together. Scamper greeted them with pleasure, and then everyone sat down and looked expectantly at Peter.

'Anything exciting?' asked Jack.

'Yes—quite,' answered Peter. 'But what about that awful sister of yours, Jack? Is she anywhere about? This is quite an important meeting.'

'No. She's gone shopping with my mother,' said Jack. 'She doesn't even *know* there's a meeting on. So we're quite safe. She won't come snooping round.'

'Have a ginger biscuit?' asked Janet, and the tin was handed round.

Peter cleared his throat. 'Well, now,' he began, 'it was my father who thought we should inquire into the matter I'm going to tell you about, so you can see it's quite important. It concerns a girl who has run away from her aunt's home, after stealing some money at school. She's been seen near here, at Belling Village, where her grandmother lives—but so far hasn't been to see her granny.'

'Oh—and I suppose it's up to the Secret Seven to keep a look-out for her—and find her!' said Jack. 'We ought to be able to do *that* all right. What's she like—and what are your plans, Peter?'

'That's just what this meeting is about,' said Peter. 'Now listen!'

The Secret Seven's Coded Message

The Secret Seven love writing secret, coded messages to one another—sometimes just for fun, but at other times so that Susie won't find out what their plans are! Here is a picture-code message which they have written specially for you. See if you can work out what it says, and then ask your friends to try. (The message is given in full on page 82.)

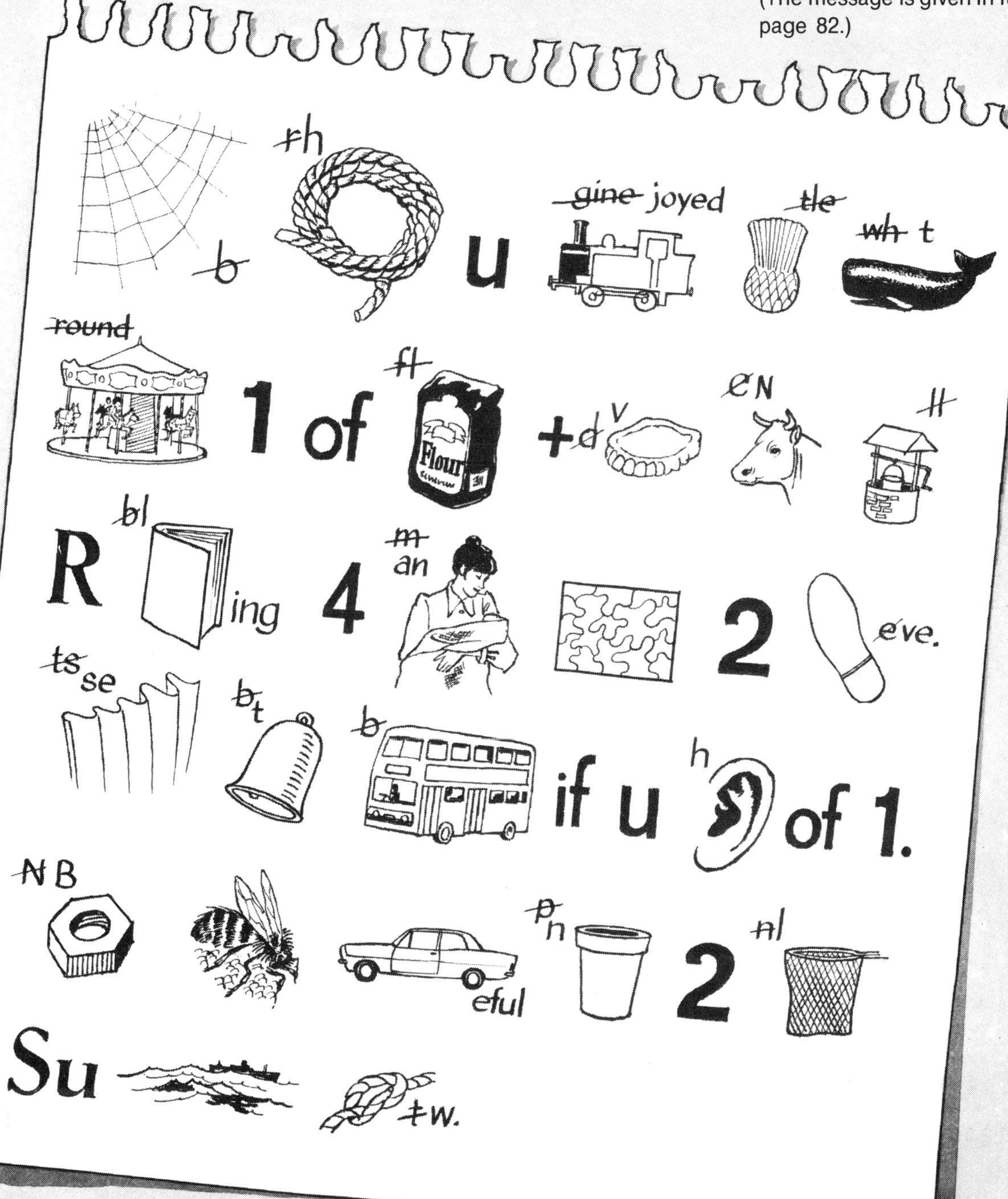

CHAPTER THREE

Mostly About Elizabeth

PETER explained everything clearly.

'The girl's name is Elizabeth Mary Wilhemina Sonning,' he said. 'Her parents live abroad, and she is a weekly boarder at school and spends her week-ends with an aunt. She has a brother who is away in France. She was accused of stealing money from her form-mistress's desk, and when the police went to speak to her aunt about it, she ran away.'

'What was she dressed in?' asked Pam.

'School uniform,' said Peter. 'Here's her photograph in it. Ordinary navy school coat, navy felt hat with school band round it, ordinary shoes, and stockings. It says here that she wore a gym tunic underneath, with a white blouse.'

'She might have taken some other clothes with her,' said Jack.

'No. Her aunt said that no other clothes were missing—only the ones she went in,' said Peter. 'You may be sure the aunt would look carefully, because it would be difficult to spot the girl if she were not in her school uniform.'

'Where's the description of what she's like?' asked Janet. 'It was in the evening paper last night, Peter.'

'Oh yes. Here it is,' said Peter, and began to read out loud. '"Elizabeth can be recognized by her mass of soft and curly hair, her brown eyes, straight eyebrows, and scar down one arm. She is tall for her age, and strong. She swims well and is fond of horses." Well—there you are—do you think you'd spot her if you saw her?'

'We might,' said Colin, doubtfully. 'But lots of girls have dark, curly hair and brown eyes. If only the girl would wear short sleeves we might spot the scar—but that's the one thing she will certainly hide!'

'How do we set about looking for her?' asked George. 'Do we bike over to Belling Village and hunt all over the place?'

'That's what we've got to discuss,' said Peter. 'I don't actually think that just biking up and down the streets is going to be the slightest good—Elizabeth will be sure to find a hiding-place. She won't wander about in the daytime, I imagine she'll lie low.'

'Where?' asked Pam.

'How do *I* know?' said Peter, who thought that Pam was sometimes very silly. 'Use your brains, Pam. Where would *you* hide if you ran away from home?'

'In a barn,' said Pam.

'In the woods under a thick bush,' said George.

'Wuff, wuff, wuff-wuff,' said Scamper.

'What did you suggest—in a *kennel*?' said Peter. 'Thank you, Scamper—quite a good idea of yours.'

Everyone laughed, and Scamper

'Here it is,' said Peter

looked very pleased.

'I thought it would be sensible if we thoroughly explored Belling Village and round about,' said Peter. 'If Elizabeth has already actually been *seen* in Belling, she must be hiding *some*where near. I expect the police have already hunted pretty well everywhere, but we know better where to look than they do—because we know where *we'd* hide if we wanted to—but they wouldn't. Grown-ups seem to forget the things they did when they were young.'

'Yes, they do,' said George. 'But I *never* shall. I'm determined not to. What about the grandmother, Peter? Should one of us go to see her, do you think? She might have something helpful to say.'

'Yes, I think that's a good idea,' said Peter, considering it.

'Bags *I* don't go,' said Pam, at once. 'I wouldn't know what to say. I should just stand there and look silly.'

'Well, you'd find *that* quite easy,' said

Peter stopped the argument before it began

Colin, and Pam scowled at him.

'Now just tell me what you—' she began, but Peter stopped the argument before it began.

'Shut up, you two. Jack and I will go, probably. And listen—there is another thing we might do.'

'What?' asked everyone.

'Well, this girl is fond of horses, it seems. We might go to the two or three stables we know of and see if any girl has been seen hanging around. She might even try to get a job at one.'

'That's a *good* idea,' said Janet, warmly. 'Well—there seems quite a lot we can do, Peter.'

'The next thing is to give each one of us a section of the countryside to hunt,' said Colin. 'It's no good us all going together—for one thing anyone in hiding would hear us coming and lie low. And for another thing we'd never cover all the countryside! What particular places must we search, Peter?'

'Well—you'll use your own common sense about that, of course,' said Peter. 'Anywhere that looks likely—a deserted shack—an empty caravan—a copse—anywhere in the woods where there are thick bushes—barns—sheds—even a hen-house!'

'Wuff, wuff, wuff-wuff,' put in Scamper.

'You mentioned a kennel before, Scamper, old thing,' said Peter. 'We'll leave *you* to examine those. Now, Secret Seven, there are two hours before dinner. Arrange between yourselves where you're going to search. Jack and I are going off to the grandmother's house. Everyone report back at half past two—SHARP! Now—get going!'

'And listen, there is another thing we might do'

CHAPTER FOUR

Jumble for Mrs Sonning

THE ADDRESS IS "BRAMBLE COTTAGE, BLACKBERRY LANE." AND REMEMBER, YOU'RE TO BE POLITE AND KIND, AND IF SHE DOESN'T WANT TO SAY A WORD ABOUT ELIZABETH, YOU ARE NOT TO ASK QUESTIONS.
MINUTES LATER, THE FRIENDS ARE READY TO LEAVE...
WASN'T THAT A BIT OF LUCK? COME ON — WE'VE GOT A WONDERFUL EXCUSE FOR CALLING ON THE OLD LADY!
IT WAS ONLY A MATTER OF MINUTES BEFORE THEY REACHED BELLING VILLAGE — AND WERE DIRECTED TO BLACKBERRY LANE...
THIS IS IT... AND THAT MUST BE THE COTTAGE!
HERE IT IS. GET YOUR JUMBLE, JACK.
SOMEONE'S COMING — I CAN HEAR FOOT-STEPS.

BUT THE WOMAN WHO OPENED THE DOOR LOOKED TOO YOUNG TO BE THE GIRL'S GRANDMOTHER...
WE HAVE BROUGHT SOME JUMBLE FOR MRS SONNING'S SALE. MAY WE SPEAK TO HER, PLEASE? I HAVE A MESSAGE FROM MY MOTHER.
COME IN— YOU CAN PUT THE BOXES DOWN IN HERE. YOU CAN'T SEE MRS SONNING — SHE'S IN BED, NOT VERY WELL. I'M MISS WARDLE, HER COMPANION, AND I'LL TELL HER YOU BROUGHT THESE.
I SUPPOSE SHE'S VERY UPSET ABOUT HER GRANDDAUGHTER. MY MOTHER WAS SORRY TO HEAR ABOUT IT TOO.
AH, YES—THE OLD LADY IS VERY TROUBLED. SHE'S SO FOND OF ELIZABETH, AND IS LONGING FOR THE CHILD TO COME TO HER. SHE DOESN'T BELIEVE ALL THAT NONSENSE ABOUT STEALING MONEY. NEITHER DO I!
DO YOU KNOW ELIZABETH, THEN?
KNOW HER! I'VE KNOWN HER SINCE SHE WAS SO HIGH! AND A NICER, MORE HONEST, STRAIGHTFORWARD CHILD I'VE NEVER SEEN. A BIT OF A RASCAL AT TIMES, BUT NONE THE WORSE FOR THAT.
POOR CHILD—I CAN'T BEAR TO THINK OF HER HIDING AWAY SOMEWHERE, AFRAID TO COME OUT.
DO YOU THINK SHE'S SOMEWHERE ABOUT HERE? SHE HAS BEEN SEEN IN THE DISTRICT, HASN'T SHE?

YES— AND, WHAT'S MORE, IT'S MY BELIEF SHE'S BEEN HERE, TO THIS VERY HOUSE! I HAVEN'T TOLD MRS SONNING ABOUT IT— IT WOULD WORRY HER. BUT SOME OF MY TARTS WENT LAST NIGHT, AND A MEAT PIE— AND A TIN OF BISCUITS! AND A RUG OFF THE SOFA!
THIS WAS NEWS INDEED! ELIZABETH MUST CERTAINLY BE IN THE DISTRICT...
WHY DO YOU SUPPOSE SHE WON'T COME TO HER GRANDMOTHER AND STAY WITH HER INSTEAD OF HIDING AWAY?
YES, PEOPLE USUALLY HIDE WHEN THEY FEEL GUILTY. BUT YOU SAY YOU DON'T BELIEVE ELIZABETH IS GUILTY OF STEALING THAT MONEY!
THAT'S TRUE— I DON'T... BUT THE PITY OF IT IS— THE MONEY WAS FOUND IN HER CHEST OF DRAWERS! SO WHAT ARE YOU TO BELIEVE?
SUDDENLY— A VOICE FROM UPSTAIRS...
WHO'S THAT, EMMA, WHO'S THAT? IS THERE ANY NEWS OF ELIZABETH?
THAT'S MRS SONNING. YOU MUST GO.
YES— MAYBE ANOTHER RUG GONE, OR A PIE! COME ON, SCAMPER— WE'VE DONE WELL!
COME ON, WE'VE GOT QUITE A LOT OF INFORMATION. AND ON MONDAY WE'LL SEE IF THERE'S ANY MORE! I'LL FIND ANOTHER BOXFUL OF JUMBLE, JACK— AND WE'LL BRING IT TO MISS WARDLE AND SEE IF SHE HAS ANYTHING MORE TO REPORT.

Horses at Work

Warner's Riding Stables is only one of several stables near Belling Village. It seems that horse riding is a popular pastime in that district, as it is in many other areas. But horses do all sorts of work apart from giving people rides. On these pages you can see some of the jobs they do—and the games they play. Can you think of any others?

Shire horses are among the largest and strongest of all horses. Farmers used to keep them for ploughing and for hauling heavy loads. Brewery companies employed them to pull special carts, called drays, on which the barrels of beer were delivered to inns. The larger brewery companies still keep Shire horses, but no longer do they have to deliver beer; nowadays they are specially groomed for display at agricultural shows and other public functions.

Show jumping is an interesting sport in which nearly everyone can take part, provided they have learned to ride properly. Competitors ride round a given course and the horses have to jump various obstacles, making as few mistakes (called 'faults') as possible. Competitions are also held for 'dressage' to see which horses are the best behaved.

As well as being clever and well-trained, circus horses have to be very elegant because the people in the audience like to admire their appearance when they are in the ring, performing under the bright spotlights. They must be calm and trustworthy too. An acrobatic rider doing somersaults and dangerous tricks must be able to trust his horse to still be beneath him when he comes down again.

Some ponies play games for a living! Polo is a popular riding sport in which two teams of four riders armed with long-handled mallets try to drive a ball between upright posts at either end of a field. The ponies have to be very agile and fast, and must learn to follow the white ball without being told.

CHAPTER FIVE

Pam and Barbara Are Busy

BUT SUDDENLY...
OH!
HEY, YOU!
AND WHAT D'YOU THINK YOU'RE DOING?
WE—WE WERE ONLY JUST WONDERING WHAT WAS IN THE SHED. WE WEREN'T DOING ANY HARM.
WELL, THAT'S THE SHED WHERE I LOCK UP MY TOOLS— LITTLE NOSEY-PARKERS! IF YOU WERE BOYS I'D GIVE YOU A HIDING!
GOODNESS— WHAT A CROSS FELLOW!
WE'D BETTER BE CAREFUL OF THE NEXT SHED WE WANT TO LOOK INTO.
YES, AND— OH, LOOK! THERE'S AN OLD CARAVAN— SEE, IN THAT FIELD UP THERE.
THAT LOOKS LIKE A GOOD PLACE FOR ANY-ONE TO HIDE IN. NOW FOR GOODNESS' SAKE LET'S BE CAREFUL THIS TIME. I'LL KEEP GUARD WHILE YOU LOOK INSIDE.
THE GIRLS MOVED IN...
PAM! SOMEONE DOES LIVE HERE! THERE ARE A COUPLE OF DIRTY OLD RUGS— OR BLANKETS—AND A TIN MUG AND PLATE. DO COME AND LOOK!

POOH! WHAT A SMELL! COME DOWN, BARBARA. YOU KNOW JOLLY WELL YOU'D NEVER HIDE IN A PLACE LIKE THIS — NOR ANY OTHER SCHOOL-GIRL EITHER. I THINK I'M GOING TO BE SICK!
YOU'RE RIGHT, I'D RATHER SLEEP IN A DITCH THAN IN THERE. DON'T BE SICK, PAM. IT'S NOT WORTH IT. COME ON, LET'S GET ON WITH OUR JOB. WE WANT TO HAVE PLENTY TO REPORT TO THE OTHERS THIS AFTERNOON.
THEY RODE ON...
...PAST A ROADMAN'S HUT...
...AND THEN THEY CAME TO A WOOD...
THORNEY-COPSE WOOD— WHAT ABOUT LOOKING IN THERE? IT HAS PLENTY OF THICK BUSHES IN IT.
YES, WE COULD GO THERE. WE'VE STILL GOT AN HOUR TO LOOK ROUND IN.
NOW LET'S BE AS QUIET AS POSSIBLE. YOU GO THAT WAY, AND I'LL GO THIS. WHISTLE TWICE IF YOU SEE ANYTHING INTERESTING.
BUT THERE WAS NOTHING TO BE SEEN— NOT EVEN A CLUE. ALL PAM FOUND WAS AN EMPTY CIGARETTE PACKET...
HMM, NOW IF THIS HAD "E.M.W.S." ON IT INSTEAD...
...AND THE ONLY THING BARBARA CAME ACROSS WAS A DIRTY HANDKERCHIEF WITH THE INITIALS "J.P." ON IT...

SUDDENLY...
OH!
QUIET! SOMEBODY'S COMING, AND IT'S A GIRL— LOOK!

THEY CREPT INTO A BUSH, AND...
YES, IT'S A SCHOOLGIRL— AND IN NAVY BLUE!
KEEP STILL— AND THEN WE'LL FOLLOW HER! I BET THAT'S THE GIRL WE WANT!

BUT SUDDENLY IT SEEMED AS THOUGH THE GIRL WAS HEADING STRAIGHT FOR THE BUSH...

SHE WAS!
OUCH!
OH!

OH, IT'S SUSIE! JACK'S HORRIBLE SISTER SUSIE! GET OFF US, SUSIE—YOU'VE NEARLY SQUASHED US FLAT. WHAT DID YOU DO THAT FOR?

WELL, YOU WERE LYING IN WAIT TO JUMP OUT AT ME, WEREN'T YOU? I SPOTTED YOU CRAWLING INTO THE BUSH!
WE WERE NOT LYING IN WAIT FOR YOU!

WELL— WHAT WERE YOU DOING, THEN? COME ON— YOU'VE GOT TO TELL ME!

Tasty Treats for Top 'Tecs

The Secret Seven love to help out in the kitchen when their mothers are cooking. Sometimes they are allowed to stir the cake mixes or roll out the pastry. And at other times they make things all by themselves with only a little assistance from their mothers. The Seven nearly all had a go at making some food for the celebration meeting at the end of this adventure. They had such fun doing so that they thought you might like to try out their recipes too. So here they have written down some of their favourite ones, and they hope you will enjoy them as much as they do. They say you must let your mother help you, though, when you need to use the cooker.

Barbara's banger rolls

You will need:

8oz (230g) plain flour
pinch of salt
2oz (55g) margarine
2oz (55g) lard
approx 2 tablespoons water
8oz (230g) sausage meat
cooking oil
little milk to glaze

Utensils:

baking tray, mixing bowl, sieve, tablespoon, rolling pin, knife, pastry brush.

Pre-heat oven to 400°F, Gas Mark 6. Brush the baking tray with a little oil.

1. Sieve the flour and salt into the mixing bowl. Rub in the margarine and lard until the mixture resembles fine breadcrumbs. Mix in the water to form a firm dough.
2. On a lightly-floured work top, roll out the pastry to an oblong about 14in (36cm) by 10in (25cm). Cut the pastry in half lengthways to make two long strips.
3. Divide the sausage meat into two equal portions. Make each portion into a long roll, the same length as the pastry strips. Put each roll of sausage meat on a pastry strip.
4. Damp the long edges of the pastry with water. Fold the pastry over the sausage meat and seal the edges together. Cut each roll into eight pieces.
5. On top of each sausage roll make three little slits for decoration, and put them on the baking tray. Brush each roll with milk.
6. Cook on second shelf from top of oven for 25-30 mins until the pastry is golden brown and the sausage meat browned.

Jack's flapjacks

You will need:

- 2 level tablespoons golden syrup
- 3oz (75g) brown sugar
- 3oz (75g) margarine
- 5oz (140g) rolled oats
- pinch of salt
- cooking oil

Utensils:

sandwich tin, thick-based saucepan, tablespoon, wooden spoon, knife.

Pre-heat oven to 325°F, Gas Mark 3. Brush the inside of the sandwich tin with oil.

1. Place the syrup, sugar and margarine in the saucepan, and put on a *low* heat until the margarine has melted and the sugar dissolved.
2. Stir with a wooden spoon and remove from the heat. Add the oats and salt to the saucepan and stir again very thoroughly.
3. Put the mixture into the tin and cook on middle shelf of oven for 15-20mins.
4. Cut the mixture into triangles while it is still hot. Leave in the tin to cool.

Pam's cheese scones

You will need:

- 8oz (230g) self-raising flour
- pinch of salt
- 2oz (55g) margarine
- 8 tablespoons milk
- 2oz (55g) grated cheese
- cooking oil
- little extra milk to glaze

Utensils:

baking tray, mixing bowl, sieve, tablespoon, rolling pin, cutter, pastry brush, wire tray.

Pre-heat oven to 450°F, Gas Mark 8. Brush the baking tray with a little oil.

1. Sieve the flour and salt into the mixing bowl. Rub the margarine into the flour with your fingertips until it resembles breadcrumbs. Add the grated cheese.
2. Make a hole in the mixture. Pour in the milk and mix until it is a smooth dough.
3. Roll out the dough on a floured surface until it is about $\frac{3}{4}$in (2cm) thick. Cut into rounds with a cutter.
4. Place the scones on the baking tray and brush with milk.
5. Cook on top shelf of oven for 7-10mins until they smell of cheese and look quite dry and golden brown on top.
6. Cool on a wire tray.

Janet's ginger cookies

You will need:

4oz (115g) plain flour cooking oil
1 rounded teaspoon ground ginger
$\frac{1}{2}$ level teaspoon baking powder
1oz (25g) brown sugar 2oz (55g) margarine
3 level tablespoons golden syrup

Utensils:

baking tray, mixing bowl, sieve, thick-based saucepan, tablespoon, teaspoon, wooden spoon.

Pre-heat oven to 325°F, Gas Mark 3. Brush the baking tray with a little oil.

1. Sieve the flour, baking powder and ginger into the mixing bowl. Make a hole in the centre of these.
2. Place the sugar, margarine and syrup in the saucepan, and put on a *low* heat until the margarine has melted and the sugar dissolved.
3. Stir the mixture with a wooden spoon and pour it into the hole in the flour. Quickly stir all the ingredients together until they are thoroughly mixed.
4. Take a teaspoon of the mixture and roll it in your hands to form a ball. Put it on the baking tray.
5. Repeat this for all the biscuits, but leave $1\frac{1}{2}$in (4cm) between each biscuit. Flatten each ball slightly.
6. Cook on middle shelf of oven for 15-20mins until golden brown.

Peter's pizza

You will need:

4oz (115g) self-raising flour 8oz (230g) tomatoes
3oz (75g) margarine 4oz (115g) cheese
1 teaspoon salt salt and pepper
4 tablespoons milk

Utensils:

pie plate, mixing bowl, sieve, wooden spoon, rolling pin, knife.

Pre-heat oven to 350°F, Gas Mark 4.

1. Sieve the flour into the mixing bowl. Rub the margarine into the flour until it is like breadcrumbs.
2. Stir the salt into the milk. Add the milk slowly to the flour, stirring all the time.
3. Knead the dough firmly on a work top for 5-10mins.
4. Form the dough into a circle and roll lightly, until it is almost the size of the pie plate. Place the dough on the pie plate and press it smooothly round the sides and bottom.
5. Slice the tomatoes and put on the dough. Sprinkle with a little salt and pepper. Slice the cheese thinly, and arrange on the tomatoes.
6. Cook on middle shelf of oven for about 35mins until the filling is cooked and the edge of the dough golden brown.

George and Colin's recipe appears on page 59

CHAPTER SIX

Up at the Stables

SO OFF THEY WENT ON THEIR BICYCLES, FEELING, AS USUAL, VERY IMPORTANT TO BE ON SECRET SEVEN WORK AGAIN. THEY CAME TO TIPTREE'S STABLES FIRST. JANET KNEW THE MAN WHO RAN IT, FOR HE WAS A FRIEND OF HER FATHER'S...

WELL — COME TO HAVE A LOOK AT MY HORSES? I'VE A FOAL IN THERE, LOOK — SILVER STAR, SHE'S CALLED, AND A BONNY THING SHE IS.

NO! I GET PLENTY OF HELP FROM MY WIFE AND TWO DAUGHTERS — THEY'RE ALL MAD ABOUT HORSES. THEY DO ALL THE WORK THERE IS TO DO — I DON'T NEED ANYONE FROM OUTSIDE. THIS IS QUITE A FAMILY STABLES!

WELL, YES, HE HAS. I ONLY JUST WONDERED IF YOU EVER GAVE JOBS TO GIRLS— LOTS OF GIRLS I KNOW LOVE HORSES AND WISH THEY COULD WORK IN A STABLES.
WHY- DID YOU THINK YOU'D COME AND HELP? YOUR FATHER HAS SURELY GOT PLENTY OF HORSES FOR YOU TO PLAY ABOUT WITH?
WE'LL GET NO USEFUL INFORMATION FROM MR TIPTREE. OBVIOUSLY THE RUNAWAY GIRL WOULDN'T BE ABLE TO GET A JOB HERE, EVEN IF SHE WANTED ONE.
COME ON, JANET.
THANK YOU FOR SHOWING US THE FOAL, MR TIPTREE. I'LL TELL MY FATHER ABOUT HER— HE'LL BE INTERESTED.
WE'LL GO TO WARNER'S STABLES NEXT. THAT'S NOT FAR FROM THE OLD GRANNY'S HOUSE. IT MIGHT BE A GOOD PLACE FOR ELIZABETH SONNING TO HIDE IN — OR GET A JOB AT.
I HARDLY THINK SHE'D GO ANYWHERE SO CLOSE, WOULD SHE? SHE MIGHT BE RECOGNISED. IT'S MORE LIKELY SHE'D GO FARTHER OFF — TO BELLING STABLES, THE OTHER SIDE OF THE VILLAGE. STILL— WE'LL GO TO WARNER'S FIRST.

WARNER'S STABLES WERE AT THE TOP OF THE NEXT HILL. GEORGE AND JANET WERE THERE WITHIN TEN MINUTES...
LET'S HAVE A SNOOP ROUND, AND IF WE SEE ANY STABLE-GIRLS, WE'LL HAVE A GOOD LOOK AT THEM.
WARNER'S STABLES
WOULDN'T ELIZABETH HAVE TO WEAR RIDING THINGS IF SHE WANTED A JOB AT A STABLE.? WE KNOW THAT SHE WAS WEARING HER SCHOOL CLOTHES WHEN SHE LEFT— SHE TOOK NO OTHERS.
WELL—SHE MIGHT HAVE BORROWED SOME AT THE STABLES. THOUGH THAT'S RATHER UNLIKELY, I THINK.
LOOK— THERE'S A STABLE-GIRL— SEE—CLEANING OUT THAT STABLE.
BUT WHEN THE GIRL TURNED ROUND...
FAR TOO BIG!
NEVER MIND. LOOK—THERE ARE TWO STABLE-BOYS OVER THERE. LET'S GO AND TALK TO THEM— WE MAY LEARN SOMETHING, YOU NEVER KNOW.

CHAPTER SEVEN

Tom Has Some News

'Hello, Janet,' said the small girl, and Janet turned in surprise

GEORGE and Janet made their way between the horses and their riders to where the two stable-boys were. One was carrying a great load of straw on his back. The other was helping a small girl down from a pony. They took no notice of George and Janet.

'Hello, Janet!' said the small girl, and Janet turned in surprise. It was Hilda, a little girl who went to her school, and was two forms below her in lessons.

'Hello, Hilda,' said Janet, feeling pleased to see her. Now she could pretend she was with her, and it wouldn't matter that she and George were not in riding clothes. Everyone would think they had come to meet Hilda.

'Thank you, Tom,' said Hilda to the

boy who had helped her down. He took the pony off to a nearby stable. Hilda followed him, accompanied by Janet and George.

'I like the other boy best,' Hilda said. 'He talks to me, but this one won't. Come and see me give my pony some sugar. He's a darling.'

They walked over to the stable with her, following Tom and the pony. The other lad had gone into the same stable with his straw, and was now spreading it on the floor of a stall. He whistled as he worked, and had a merry look in his eye.

'You talk to this boy, and I'll talk to the other one,' said George, in a low voice to Janet. 'Talk to Hilda too—find out if any new girl is here helping in any way—or if she has seen any strange girl wandering about, watching, as we are doing.'

'Right,' said Janet, and went to Tom and Hilda.

'It must be fun working with horses,' she said to the boy, who was now fastening the pony to the wall. He nodded.

'Not bad,' he said.

'It's funny that so many more girls ride than boys,' went on Janet. 'I can't see a single boy here except you and the other stable-boy. Are there any others?'

'No,' said the boy. 'Just us two.' He began to clean out the stall next to the little pony, turning his back on Hilda and Janet. Janet thought he was rather rude. So did Hilda.

'He's like that,' she whispered to Janet. 'The other boy, Harry, doesn't mind telling you anything. He's talking to George as if he's known him for years.'

So he was. George was getting on very well indeed!

'Do they have many stable-girls here?' George asked, when he had a good chance. The burly fellow shook his head.

'Only one—and she's over there. One came the other day to ask for a job, but Mr Warner turned her down at once. Why, she wasn't any bigger than you! And yet she said she could handle this big cob over there.'

George pricked up his ears. He wasn't interested in the cob, but he was interested in this girl who had come for a job! Could it have been Elizabeth?

'What was she like?' he asked. Harry called across to the other stable-boy.

'Hey, Tom—what was that girl like who came and asked for a job the other day?'

'Was she brown-eyed?' asked George, eagerly. 'Had she masses of dark, fluffy hair? And did you notice if she had a scar down one of her arms?'

The stable-boy swung round sharply and stared at George. 'What girl's that?' he asked. 'Is she a friend of yours?'

'No, not exactly,' said George. 'It's—er—well, it's just someone we're looking out for. Do tell me, was this girl like my description of her?'

'I didn't see her,' said Tom, much to Janet's and George's disappointment. 'I wasn't here the day she came.'

'Oh, no—that's right,' said Harry. 'Well, I know she hadn't got dark hair—she had yellow hair, and she was lively as a monkey. Very cross too, when Mr Warner turned her down. She couldn't have been your friend.'

'I saw a girl like the one you described when I was in Gorton the other day,'

'Tom! I want you!' called a voice and Mr Warner looked into the stable

said Tom suddenly. 'Mass of fluffy brown hair, you said, didn't you—and a scar down one arm.'

'Did you? Did you *really* see her?' cried Janet, coming up, looking thrilled. Now they were really getting warm! 'How did you manage to see her scar?'

'Oh—she sat in a tea-shop, and it was hot there—so she took off her coat,' said Tom. 'I saw her scar then.'

'But hadn't she a long-sleeved school blouse on?' asked Janet, surprised.

'Maybe. But her sleeves must have been rolled up if so,' said Tom, and bent to his work again.

'Tom—this is really very important,' said George, joining in. 'Could you tell us anything she said—did she speak to you?'

'She said she was going to catch a train to London and see if she could fly to France to join a brother of hers,' said Tom, to Janet's and George's surprise and excitement. Why, the girl *must* have been Elizabeth, then. A scar on her arm—and a brother in France! There was no doubt about it!

'Tom! I want you!' called a voice, and Mr Warner looked into the stable. 'Come and show this child how to saddle her horse.'

Tom went off, and Janet and George looked at one another, delighted. 'Well—we've got something to report to the meeting this afternoon!' said Janet. 'Come on, George—we needn't stay here any longer.'

Keep that Bike Moving

The Secret Seven would be lost without their bikes—they need them for getting around their district, especially when they've an important assignment, like the one they're working on in this annual. So they make sure they keep their machines in tip-top condition.

If you have a bike you'll want it always to be roadworthy—and here are a few tips which the Seven would like to pass on to you. Remember, they say, that 'prevention is better than cure': taking good care of your bike and watching for signs of trouble will pay off. Regular routine checks and prompt attention to any problem will mean that your bike will always be in working order and safe to ride. So study the tips below, put them into practice—and keep that bike moving!

Bell. Oil regularly. Keep positioned so that, when ringing, you can still control your bike and apply the brakes.

Brake blocks and mechanism. Check blocks regularly for wear. Replace when worn. Keep mechanism adjusted; blocks should remain close to wheel-rims when brakes are off. Replace fraying brake cables.

Handlebar. Maintain at right height —grips level with front of saddle.

Saddle. Keep tightly locked in position, tilted very slightly upward. From saddle, you should be able to touch the ground firmly with your toes. Adjust if necessary.

Carrier. Never carry objects in your hand while riding; fit and use a carrier or saddle-bag. If cycling any distance, ensure bag contains puncture outfit, including tyre levers.

Front lamp. Keep clean. Ensure mounting is kept tight to prevent lamp moving about.

Steering head. Keep adjusted to avoid 'shake'.

Dynamo. Keep adjusted so that maximum power is obtained.

Pump. Keep in working order and fasten securely in position.

Rear lamp. Keep clean. Ensure mounting is tight to prevent mobility: lamp must face directly to the rear.

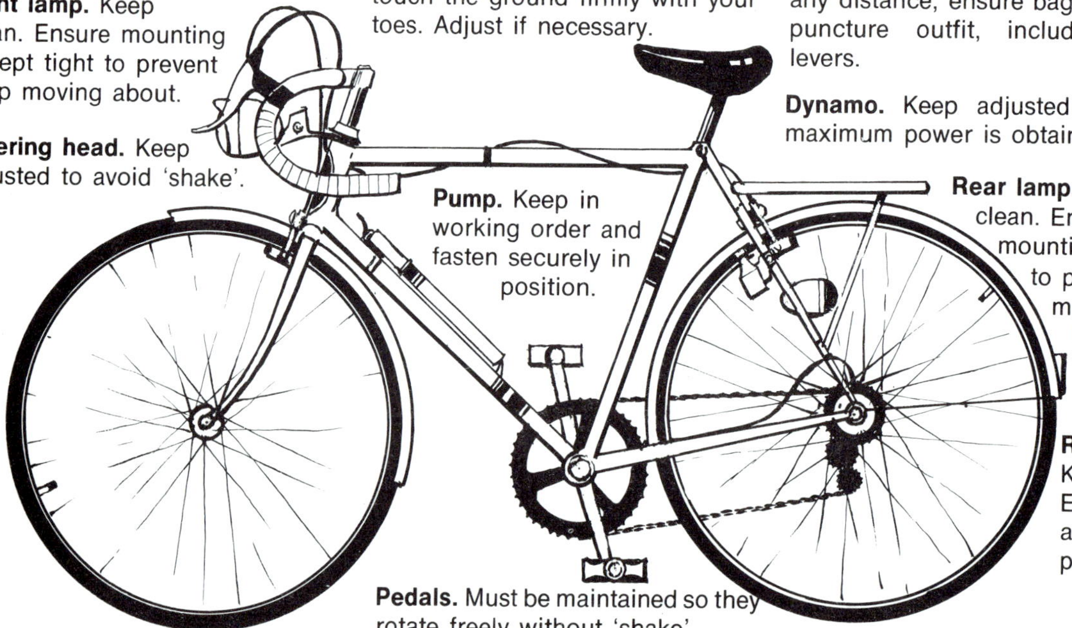

Reflector. Keep clean. Ensure nuts are tight to prevent loss.

Pedals. Must be maintained so they rotate freely without 'shake'.

Front forks. Bent forks are dangerous. If bent, have forks straightened or replaced.

Chain. Keep lightly greased. Ensure there is no more than ¾" 'play' midway along the chain. To tighten, loosen wheel nuts and pull wheel back as necessary. Adjust brakes at same time.

Wheel hubs (front and rear). Keep 'cones' adjusted to prevent 'shake'. Wheel nuts to be kept tight.

Mudguards. Keep all nuts tight. Replace broken stays.

Tyres. Replace if badly worn. Watch for weaknesses, indicated by swelling. If this happens, investigate—it may be the tube that's at fault. Keep tyres pumped up 'hard'.

Spokes. If broken, replace. Keep tightly adjusted with use of special 'spoke key'.

If problems arise which are not covered by the above, get them attended to by a specialist. And remember—an uncared-for machine can be an unsafe machine.

CHAPTER EIGHT

Another Meeting

EVERYONE was early for the two-thirty meeting, and the password was muttered five times as Janet and Peter opened and shut the door of the shed. Scamper barked a welcome to everyone. Then the door was locked and the meeting began.

'I hope everyone has something to report,' said Peter. 'I'll begin with my report. Well, Jack and I went to the grandmother's house, but the old lady wasn't well, so we didn't see her. We didn't find it difficult to ask questions, and her companion was quite friendly.'

'That was a bit of luck!' said George.

'It was,' said Peter. 'We learnt quite a few things—for instance, that Elizabeth is definitely hiding somewhere in the district—not far from her granny's, I should think—because she has got into the house at night and taken pies and things, and an old rug!'

George and Janet looked astonished. 'But, Peter—' began George and Janet together. Peter frowned. 'Please don't interrupt,' he said. 'You and Janet can have your say in a minute. Well, as I was saying—the old lady's companion, Miss Wardle, told us quite a lot about Elizabeth, and said that she was a very nice, straightforward girl.'

'She can't be!' interrupted Pam. 'You can't call a thief straightforward! She was only just *saying* that!'

'Be quiet,' said Peter, exasperated.

George and Janet looked astonished

'The point I'm trying to make is that there's no doubt that Elizabeth is hiding somewhere near her grandmother's —and getting food from there. And she'll do that at night as often as she needs food! I suggest that we go and watch one night, and see if we can catch her. Jack and I are going to take some more jumble to the grandmother's on Monday, and if Elizabeth has been getting into the house again, we could perhaps watch that night.'

'Yes. Jolly good idea!' said Pam, Barbara, and Colin. George and Janet said nothing, but looked meaningly at one another.

'Well, that's my report—mine and Jack's,' said Peter. 'What about you, Colin?'

'Nothing to report at all,' said Colin, in a rather apologetic tone. 'I examined about six sheds, all kinds of barns, and wandered over a whole caravan colony the other side of Belling Hill—but didn't find out a thing. Not a thing. I'm sorry, Peter.'

'That's all right,' said Peter. 'You and Pam, Barbara—what's your report?'

'Well, nothing much, either,' said Barbara. 'We looked in a locked shed—or tried to—and got turned off by a man with a horse. And we found a terribly smelly old caravan with a rug inside and a tin cup and plate. And we hunted all through Thorney-Copse Wood, looking into and under bushes.'

'And that awful sister of Jack's was there, too,' said Pam. 'We saw her coming along, dressed in the same uniform as we wear—navy blue coat and hat—and we thought it might be the runaway girl, so we hid in a bush—and

Susie jumped right into it on purpose and fell on top of us—you should see the bruise I've got!'

'So *that's* why Susie was pestering the life out of me at dinner to find out what the Secret Seven are up to!' said Jack. 'You *are* a couple of idiots to make her think there is something up, you two. Now I shan't have a moment's peace. Susie is bound to find out what we're after—she's as sharp as a needle.'

'She certainly is,' said Peter, who had a healthy respect for Susie's sharpness. 'I wouldn't be a bit surprised if she's not snooping outside somewhere now, listening for all she's worth.'

'Scamper would bark,' began Janet—and just at that very moment Scamper *did* bark as a face looked in at

Jack raced out with Scamper at his heels

the window of the shed! It was Susie, of course.

'Hello, Secret Seven,' she called. 'I *thought* you'd be here, Jack. I know what you're all up to. I found your newspaper cutting! Ha, ha.'

Peter looked furiously at Jack. 'Do you mean to say you left that newspaper report about?' he said.

'That's right, tick him off!' said the annoying Susie, pressing her face closer to the window. 'I say, you do look a lot of sweetie-pies sitting down there. Shall I tell you my news of Elizabeth Mary Wilhemina Sonning?'

Jack leapt up in a fury, flung open the door, and raced out with Scamper at his heels. The others went to the door.

Susie was a fast runner. She was running out of the gate, laughing, before Jack was half-way there. He knew it was no good chasing after her. He went back to the shed, red in the face.

'Do you suppose she heard what we were all saying?' asked Jack. Peter shook his head.

'No. Scamper would have barked. Susie could only just that moment have come. I must say it's very annoying. Now Susie will be hunting too. Blow! If she finds Elizabeth before we do, I shall be jolly furious.'

'She won't,' said George, bursting to tell what he had heard from Tom the stable-boy. 'You just wait till you hear what Janet and I have to report.'

Make a Paper Scamper

Do you like making paper models? The Secret Seven do—and they've invented a model just for you! It's a paper Scamper, and it's very easy to make and fun to have around. Peter and Janet say it's not *all* that good a likeness of their lovable dog, for Scamper's ears don't really cover his eyes. But it seems Scamper quite likes it—when Peter showed it to him, he tried to eat it!

Here's how you can make your own paper Scamper:

Take a piece of paper about 25cm square, and fold it in half.

Push in the fold from a fifth of the way from the bottom to the opposite corner (figs. 1 & 2).

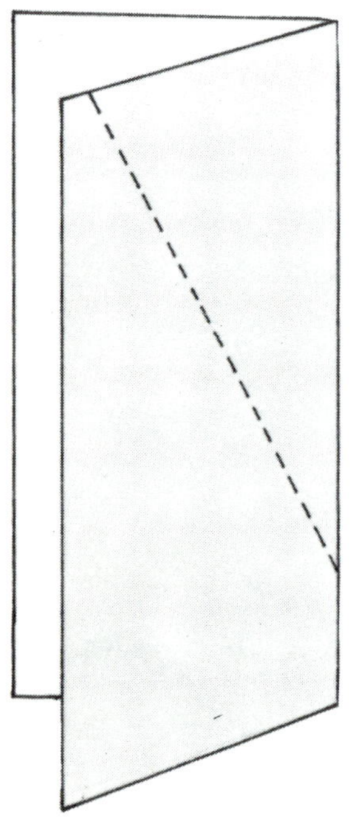

Fig. 1

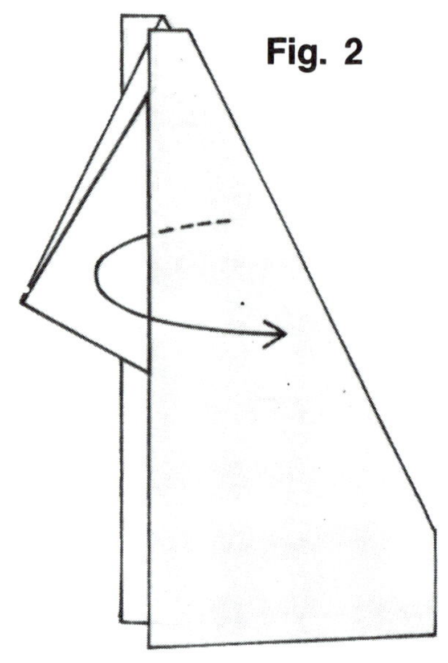

Fig. 2

Fig. 3

Pull down the corner at 'A' on each side (figs. 2 & 3).

Push in the nose at 'B'.

Pleat the paper on each side at 'C' (figs. 3 & 4).

Push in the tail at 'D', and fold out the bottom edge on each side so that Scamper sits comfortably (figs. 4 & 5). And don't forget to draw in his nose and mouth!

Once you have mastered Scamper, see what else you can make from paper, such as a boat or a lantern. Or borrow a book from the library which shows you how to make different types of paper models. You may find this under the subject of Origami, which is the name given to the ancient Japanese art of paper-folding.

With practice and patience you will soon be making all sorts of paper animals, birds, ships . . . and perhaps even models from your own designs!

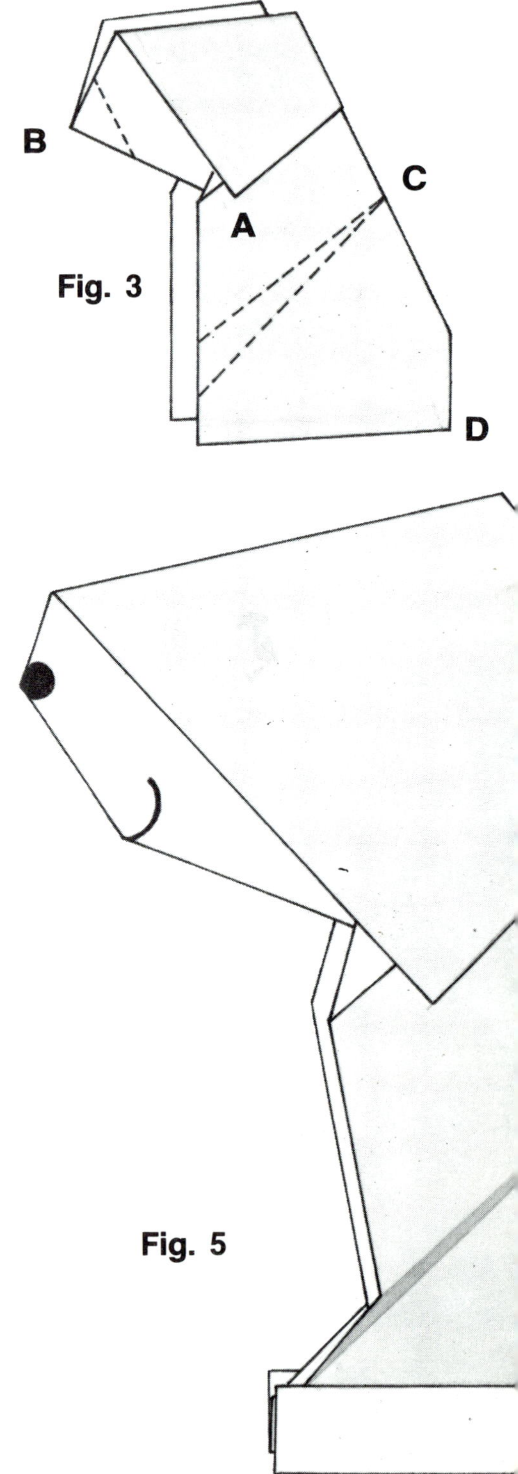

Fig. 5

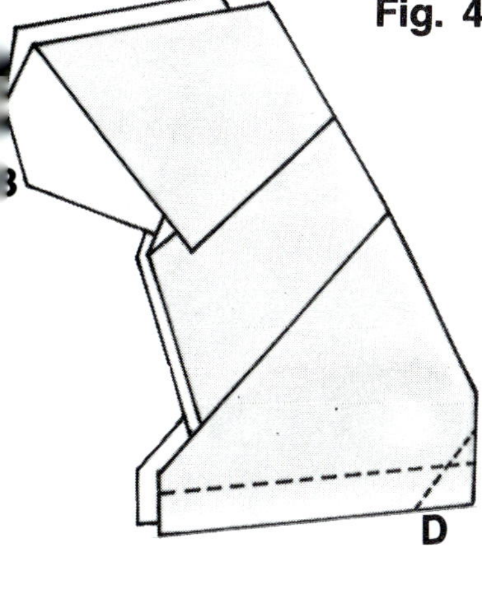

How do You Rate?

Would *you* make a good Secret Seven member? If you're sharp-eyed, quick-witted and have 'staying power', probably you would, for these are the three most important factors which each member of the Seven possesses. Below are some simple tests designed to assess your abilities.

See how well you can do, remembering that each member of the Seven passed these tests with flying colours! Check your answers with those on page 82.

TOWN JUMBLE

Below are the names of 20 towns and cities, but each one has been broken in two and the halves jumbled up. For example, Blackpool and Portsmouth have been mixed up to make Blackmouth and Portspool. Can you unscramble the others? (Score 20 points if all answers are correct.)

BLACKMOUTH	**GLASCASTLE**
BRISTRY	**SWANBOROUGH**
LONINGHAM	**MANBURGH**
EXING	**PORTSPOOL**
NEWGOW	**WINDCOLN**
EDINCHESTER	**BORNEPOOL**
SCARSEA	**COVENTOL**
BRIGHFORD	**BIRMDON**
LIVERMOUTH	**READETER**
LINSOR	**BRADTON**

TRUE OR FALSE?

Here are 10 statements based on the Secret Seven story in this annual. Are they true or false? You will need to have read the whole story before you can answer all the questions—although you *could* find the answers by quickly checking the relevant chapters.

1. Peter and Janet were having dinner when their father first told them of Elizabeth's disappearance. *True or False?* (Chapter 1)

2. The Seven's password for their first meeting to discuss searching for Elizabeth was 'Mint Sauce'. *True or False?* (Chapter 2)

3. Mrs Sonning lived at Blackberry Cottage, Bramble Lane. *True or False?* (Chapter 4)

4. Pam and Barbara went to explore the woods and fields on the east side of Belling. *True or False?* (Chapter 5)

5. When George and Janet first went to Warner's Stables, Janet recognised a girl dismounting from a pony. It was her friend Hilda. *True or False?* (Chapter 7)

6. When Susie turned up at the Seven's meeting place to tell them she knew what they were investigating, Peter chased her away. *True or False?* (Chapter 8)

7. It was on a Tuesday evening that Jack and Peter took a second box of jumble to Mrs Sonning. *True or False?* (Chapter 10)

8. The suitcase bearing the initials E.M.W.S. was found at the foot of a flight of stone steps in an old cottage. *True or False?* (Chapter 12)

9. Peter told Tom to hoot if he heard anyone coming while they were hiding outside Mrs Sonning's cottage. *True or False?* (Chapter 13)

10. Charles, Elizabeth's brother, came over from Holland to see if he could help find Elizabeth. *True or False?* (Chapter 16)

(Score 10 points if all answers are correct.)

There are more 'How do you rate?' tests on page 78

CHAPTER NINE

Reports and Plans

'GIVE your report, George and Janet,' said Peter. 'It sounds as if it may be an important one.'

'It is,' said Janet, proudly. 'You begin, George.'

'Well,' began George, 'Janet and I went to Tiptree Stables first, but as they don't employ anyone there except their own family, we knew Elizabeth wouldn't have got a job there. So we left at once and went on to Mr Warner's stables.'

'And we saw a stable-girl there, but she was much too big to be Elizabeth,' put in Janet.

'Then we saw two stable-boys—one a big, burly fellow called Harry, and the other smaller, called Tom. He was a bit surly, we thought, but Harry wasn't. He was nice. We asked him if any girl had been asking for a job at Mr Warner's, and one had, but she had yellow hair not brown, so we knew that was no good.'

'And when we told Harry what the girl was like that we wanted, the other boy, Tom, who was listening, suddenly said that *he* had seen a girl like the one we were describing—and she even had a scar down one arm!' cried Janet, unable to resist joining in.

'What!' cried everyone.

'This *is* news,' said Peter, delighted. 'Go on, George. Where had he seen Elizabeth—because it must be her if the description tallies.'

'This *is* news,' said Peter, delighted. 'Go on, George'

'He said he met her in a tea-shop in Gorton—that's not very far from here, is it? She was having tea, I suppose. It was hot and she had her coat off—that's how he noticed the scar down one arm. She talked to him.'

'What did she say?' demanded Peter, his eyes shining.

'She told him she was going to London to see if she could get a plane to fly to France to see her brother,' said Janet. 'She did really! So it *must* have been Elizabeth, mustn't it?'

'Yes. Of course it must,' said Peter, and the others nodded their heads. A brother in France—a scar on one arm—it *could* only be Elizabeth.

'Well, now you see why Janet and I don't think that Elizabeth is hiding anywhere in the district,' said George. 'She's probably hiding somewhere in London, trying to find out about planes.'

'Well—can you answer this question then, if that's so?' said Peter, looking suddenly puzzled. 'If Elizabeth is in London, waiting to fly to France, who is it who is taking pies and a rug from her grandmother's house at night?'

There was a deep silence.

Everyone looked at Peter, even Scamper.

'I hadn't thought of that,' said Janet. 'Well, of course, George and I didn't know anything about the pies till you told us in your report, Peter. Blow! One of our reports is wrong somehow. If Elizabeth is hanging round her granny's house at night, she can't be going to fly to France!'

'She might have found that she hadn't enough money to get to London and buy a seat on a plane,' said Jack. 'She might

Peter made up his mind to go and interview the two stable-boys himself

have changed her mind and gone to Belling, after all. She might even have hoped to get money from her grandmother's house. After all, if she had stolen once, she could easily do so again.'

'That's true,' said Peter. 'Yes—I think you're right, Jack. She may have made that plan at the beginning and then found she hadn't enough money—and so she came to this district. We know she was seen somewhere about here.'

There was another silence. The Seven were trying to sort things out in their minds. 'What about that girl who came to ask Mr Warner for a job—the one Harry told you about,' said Janet to George. 'He said she had golden hair, didn't he? Well, I suppose she might have had it dyed, mightn't she—I mean, that *might* have been Elizabeth, after all. I know my auntie once had her hair dyed golden when it was brown. So Elizabeth could have done the same, couldn't she?'

Nobody knew very much about hair being dyed, and Peter made up his mind that the next thing to do was to go and interview the two stable-boys himself. They might be able to tell him something they hadn't thought of telling Janet or George.

'I shall go and see those boys,' he said. 'What are they like to look at?'

'I told you Harry was big and burly, and the other smaller,' said George. 'They've both got dark hair, rather untidy. They ought to exchange riding-breeches too—Harry's are too small for him, and Tom's are too large! Wasn't it a bit of luck Tom meeting Elizabeth at Gorton—now we know for certain she must be somewhere about, still wearing her school things.'

'Well, she's *got* to be somewhere near, or she couldn't raid her granny's house at night,' said Peter. 'Now, what do we do next? Tomorrow's Sunday, we can't do anything then. It will have to be Monday after school.'

'You and I will go to old Mrs Sonning's with more jumble,' said Jack, 'and find out the latest news from *that* quarter.'

'And after that we'll go and see the stable-boys,' said Peter. 'The others can come too, so that it won't seem too noticeable, us asking questions. Meet here at five o'clock on Monday. Well—I *hope* we're on the trail—but it's not very easy at the moment!'

CHAPTER TEN

Miss Wardle Has More News

'That's just what I was thinking,' said Peter

SUNDAY passed rather slowly.

When Peter and Janet came back from morning church, Peter had an idea.

'Janet—Jack and I are going to take some more jumble to old Mrs Sonning tomorrow, you remember—to make an excuse for asking about Elizabeth again—so shall we hunt up some? What sort of things does Mother give for jumble? Old clothes mostly, I suppose.'

'Yes. But we can't give away any of our clothes without asking her,' said Janet. 'And she would want to know why we were doing it—she'd guess it was an excuse to go to old Mrs Sonning again, and she might not approve.'

'That's just what I was thinking,' said Peter. 'I know—let's turn out our cupboards and see if there's anything we can find that would do for jumble.'

They found plenty! It was astonishing what a lot of things they had which they

'And look, here are my old sandals'

had quite forgotten about and never used.

'Two packs of snap cards,' said Peter. 'A game of snakes and ladders—we've never even *used* it, because we always preferred our old game. And look here—a perfectly new ball! Shall we give that?'

'Well, jumble isn't really supposed to be *new* things,' said Janet. 'Let's give our old ball instead. And look, here are my old sandals I thought I'd left at the seaside! I can't get into them now—they can go.'

In the end they had quite a big box full of jumble and felt very pleased with themselves. They longed for Monday to come!

It came at last, and then there was morning school to get through, and afternoon school as well. They raced home to tea and were down in the shed just before five o'clock. All the Seven were there, very punctual indeed!

'Good,' said Peter, pleased. 'Well, Jack and I will bike to Bramble Cottage, and see if we can get any more news out of Miss Wardle, the companion, or Mrs Sonning, the granny. The rest of you can bike up to Warner's Stables and wait for us there. Chat to the stable-boys all you can. We'll join you later.'

They all set off, Peter with a neat box of 'jumble' tied to the back of his bicycle. They parted at the top of Blackberry Lane, and Jack and Peter went down the winding road, while the others rode up the hill to where Warner's Stables were right at the top.

Peter and Jack left their bicycles at the gate of Bramble Cottage and went to the front door. They knocked, hoping that Miss Wardle would come, not old Mrs Sonning. Mrs Sonning might not be so willing to talk about Elizabeth as Miss Wardle was!

Thank goodness it was the companion who opened the door again. She seemed quite pleased to see them.

'Well now—don't say you've been kind enough to bring us some *more* jumble!' she said. 'Mrs Sonning was *so* pleased with the boxes you brought on Saturday. I'll give her these—she's still in bed, dear old lady.'

'Oh, I'm sorry,' said Peter. 'Hasn't she heard any more of her granddaughter?'

'Not a word,' said Miss Wardle. 'The police say she seems to have disappeared completely—and yet she came here again last night—*and* the night before!'

This was indeed news! 'Did she?' asked Peter eagerly. 'Did you see her?

She seemed quite pleased to see them

'What? Watch every door and window?' said the companion

Did she leave a note?'

'No. Not a note, not even a sign that she was here,' said Miss Wardle, 'except that more food was gone. How she got in beats me. Every door and window I made fast myself. She must have got a key to the side-door. That's the only one with no bolt.'

'What do the police say about that?' asked Jack.

'Nothing,' said Miss Wardle, rather indignantly. 'It's my belief they think I'm making it up, they take so little notice. Why don't they put a man to watch the house at night—they'd catch the poor child then, and what a relief it would be to the old lady to know she was safe!'

'They probably *do* put a man to watch,' said Peter, 'but I expect Elizabeth knows some way into the house that they don't. I bet she knows if there's a policeman about—and where he is and everything. *I* would! Why don't *you* watch, Miss Wardle?'

'What? Watch every door and window?' said the companion. 'Nobody could do that. And I'm not one to be able to keep awake all night, even if I had to.'

'Well—we'd better go,' said Peter. 'I *do* hope Elizabeth is soon found. It must be awful hiding away in some cold, lonely place all by herself, not daring to come home because she feels ashamed.'

They said good-bye and went. 'Well,' said Peter, as soon as they were out of the front gate, 'I know what *I'm* going to do tonight! I'm going to hide somewhere in the garden here! I bet I'll see Elizabeth if she comes—but I shan't tell the police. I'll try and get her to go and tell everything to her granny!'

'Good idea! I'll come too!' said Jack, thrilled. 'Let's go up to the stables now and find the others. I bet they'll want to come and watch as well!'

The Hunt is On

Hidden in the picture are a number of objects Elizabeth would find useful if she was in hiding near Bramble Cottage. Can you help her to hunt them out? There is a torch, penknife, mug, pie, cake, bottle of milk, comb and a watch.

Then hunt for all the mistakes in the passage beneath the picture. There are ten mistakes in all.

Bramble Cottage is a pretty little house in Gorton Village. It is the home of Elizabeth's aunt, Mrs Wardle, and her companion, Miss Sonning. When Peter and Colin first called there with some jumble for the church sale, they learnt that some fruit, biscuits and buns had disappeared from the kitchen the night before. More food had gone by the time the boys returned to the cottage three days later. So Peter and George decided that they would keep watch on Bramble Cottage the next day.

Solution on page 82

CHAPTER ELEVEN

Tom - and a Bit of Excitement

WE SHALL BE THERE AT HALF PAST TEN— NOT THE GIRLS— JUST THE FOUR BOYS. I'LL GIVE AN OWL-HOOT WHEN WE ARRIVE— AND IF YOU'RE THERE, HOOT BACK.

APPARENTLY THEY DID, AND A LONG TRAIL OF CHILDREN RIDING OR LEADING THE PONIES WENT OVER THE HILL AND DOWN TO THE FIELDS, BRIGHT IN THE EVENING SUN...

SOON TOM AND HARRY SAID GOOD-BYE, AND THE SEVEN COLLECTED THEIR BICYCLES...
COME ON, LET'S TAKE THE HILL-PATH...
GOOD IDEA, JACK. IT'S A BIT BUMPY, MIND. HOLD ON TIGHT, GIRLS!
WARNER'S STABLES
THEY WERE NEARING THE BOTTOM OF THE HILL, WHEN...
HEY, LOOK—STRAIGHT AHEAD!
IS THAT ELIZABETH—WITH A SUIT-CASE, TOO! QUICK, LET'S FOLLOW!
LOOK—WHAT'S THAT ON THE GROUND BY THE STILE? PERHAPS IT'S SOMETHING SHE DROPPED!
A HANDKERCHIEF! AND LOOK—IT'S GOT 'E' IN THE CORNER! IT WAS ELIZABETH! HER HIDING-PLACE IS SOME-WHERE NEAR HERE. QUICK, LET'S FOLLOW HER.
AS THEY LIFTED THEIR BICYCLES OVER THE STILE...
THERE SHE IS—AT THE CORNER—BY THAT OLD COTTAGE!
IF ONLY WE CAN GET HER TO BE FRIENDS AND COME WITH US! RING YOUR BELLS, ALL OF YOU, SO THAT SHE'LL HEAR US COMING!

Quick Tricks and Teasers

When the Secret Seven aren't out on a special assignment, there's nothing they like better than having fun with quick tricks and teasers. On this page they show you some simple ones with which you can entertain your friends.

AMAZING MATCHSTICKS!

Ask your mother for a number of used matchsticks and share them amongst your friends—say, five each. (*Never* use matches which have not already been struck; you could give yourself a nasty burn.) Fill a bowl with water and challenge your friends to drop their matchsticks into the bowl so that they float upright. They'll find it impossible—matches *never* float upright!

Now it's your turn. First you drop in a couple of matchsticks which float like all the others . . . your friends will think it's too difficult for *you* too! But then you drop in a matchstick which *does* float upright—and then another . . .

How is it done?

Before your friends arrive push a short pin into the end of each of the matchsticks which you want to float upright. The weight of the pin is the secret of your amazing matchsticks!

PUZZLING PYRAMID

Can you turn this pyramid the right way up by moving only three of the spots? Sounds easy? Just let your friends try! When they give up, show them how it's done.

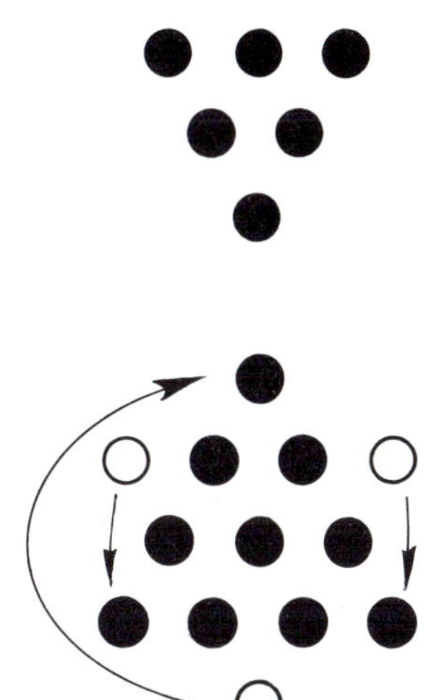

MATCH MYSTERY

Arrange 12 used matches as shown below and ask your friends to move them about so that, still using the same number of matches, they are left with three squares instead of four.

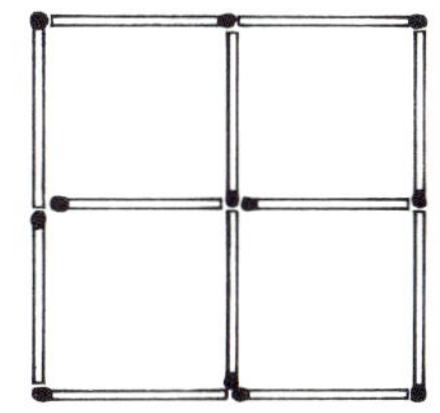

It's a tricky one, this! Here's the answer:

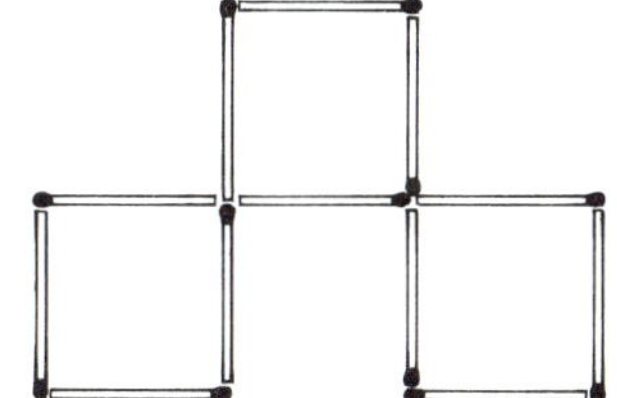

STANDING INSIDE A POSTCARD

When you ask your friends to try standing inside a postcard they'll think you're joking—but it *can* be done. Here's how:

Take an ordinary postcard and fold it in half. Then cut it as shown below. If you follow the diagram exactly you'll be able to open up the postcard to produce a long, thin circle of card—which you can lay on the floor and stand inside!

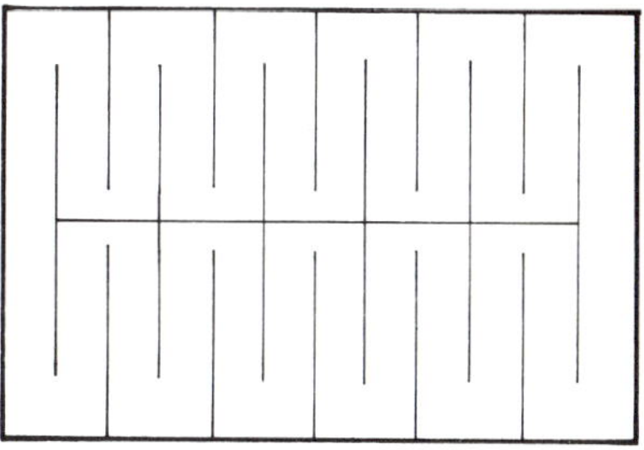

The Secret Seven have set this special word hunt puzzle for you. Tackle it when you've finished reading the story and see how many of the answers you can recall from memory—or set out on the trail right away and hunt out the answers from the chapters indicated at the end of the questions. The number of words, and the letters in those words, are clearly indicated for you after the chapter numbers.

The Seven have formed the puzzle in such a way that, beginning in the top left-hand corner and moving in a clockwise direction, the last letter of the first word is also the first letter of the second word, and so on.

If you are unable to solve any of the clues, the answers are printed upside down at the foot of the page. Happy hunting!

Word Hunt

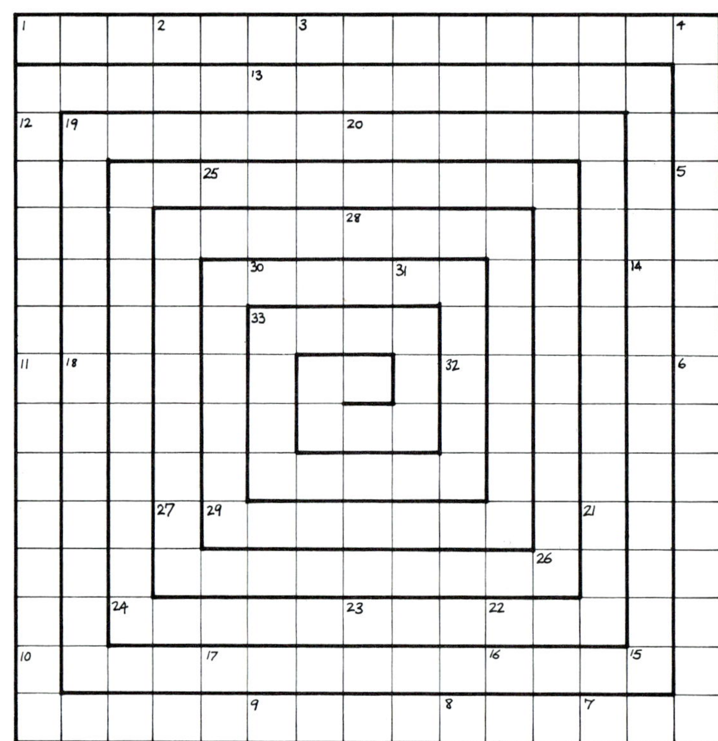

CLUES

1. Where the money was stolen from. *(Chapter 1) (4)*
2. Name of the stable-girl who worked with Tom and Harry. *(Chapter 17) (4)*
3. Who was thought to have taken tarts from Bramble Cottage? *(Chapter 4) (9)*
4. What noise was Tom to make if he heard anyone in the garden of Bramble Cottage? *(Chapter 13) (4)*
5. What did the farm labourer keep locked in his shed? *(Chapter 5) (5)*
6. What was the name of the foal at Tiptree's Stables? *(Chapter 6) (6,4)*
7. There were two of these in the old caravan. *(Chapter 5) (4)*
8. What Harry was carrying the first time George and Janet saw him. *(Chapter 7) (5)*
9. Which stables did George and Janet visit after Tiptree's? *(Chapter 6) (7)*
10. Elizabeth's surname. *(Chapter 1) (7)*
11. Where Tom said he had seen a girl who fitted Elizabeth's description. *(Chapter 7) (6)*
12. Janet wrote these to the members of the Secret Seven to call them to a meeting. *(Chapter 1) (7)*
13. What Elizabeth was pictured wearing in the newspaper. *(Chapter 1) (6,7)*
14. The password which Janet couldn't remember. *(Chapter 2) (4,5)*
15. The initials on the suitcase found at the top of the stone stairs. *(Chapter 12) (4)*
16. Scamper is a golden .... *(Chapter 1) (7)*
17. Who owned up to the theft and cleared Elizabeth? *(Chapter 16) (4,6)*
18. Where Elizabeth was going to take a train to, according to Tom. *(Chapter 7) (6)*
19. What was inside the suitcase, apart from a small

George and Colin's toffee apples

You will need:

- 6 eating apples
- 8oz (230g) granulated sugar
- 1 teaspoon golden syrup
- ¼pt (140ml) water
- pinch of cream of tartar
- cooking oil

Utensils:

baking tray, 6 wooden skewers, thick-based saucepan, teaspoon, cup.

Brush the baking tray with a little oil.

1. Wash and dry the apples. Stick a skewer into the top of each one.
2. Put the sugar, golden syrup, water and cream of tartar into the saucepan, and put on a *low* heat until the sugar has dissolved.
3. Increase the heat and boil the mixture for about 20 mins until it is golden brown.
4. Remove from the heat. Drop a small amount of the mixture into a cup of cold water. The toffee should form a hard ball if it is ready.
5. Dip each apple into the toffee very carefully. Place on the baking tray and leave to set.

box tied with string? *(Careful—this is a trick question!) (Chapter 12) (7)*

20. Janet's mother gave her a tin of these for the Seven to eat at their meeting. *(Chapter 2) (6,8)*
21. Who called the Seven 'a lot of sweetie-pies'? *(Chapter 8) (5)*
22. Miss Wardle's first name. *(Chapter 4) (4)*
23. This relation of Janet had her hair dyed golden. *(Chapter 9) (6)*
24. What did Pam spot in a field after she and Barbara had explored a shed? *(Chapter 5) (5,7)*
25. What did Susie find which told her what the Seven were 'up to'? *(Chapter 8) (9,7)*
26. Jack hid beside this in the garden of Bramble Cottage. *(Chapter 13) (6,4)*
27. Having explored the caravan, what did Pam and Barbara see which may have made a good hiding place, had it not been occupied? *(Chapter 5) (8,3)*
28. Where did Barbara find a handkerchief bearing the initials J.P.? *(Chapter 5) (7-5,4)*
29. Lucy placed the stolen cash-box in Elizabeth's chest of .... *(Chapter 16) (7)*
30. According to the newspaper report, what mark did Elizabeth have down one arm? *(Chapter 3) (4)*
31. Elizabeth went to this aunt's home during the weekend following the theft. *(Chapter 16) (4)*
32. What Tom was doing with the ponies on the last evening that the Seven went up to Warner's Stables. *(Chapter 18) (10)*
33. In what condition was the farm labourer's shed which Pam and Barbara investigated? *(Chapter 5) (4,6)*

Answers

1. Desk 2. Kate 3. Elizabeth 4. Hoot 5. Tools 6. Silver Star 7. Rugs 8. Straw 9. Warner's 10. Sonning 11. Gorton 12. Notices 13. School uniform 14. Mint sauce 15. E.M.W.S. 16. Spaniel 17. Lucy Howell 18. London 19. Nothing! 20. Ginger biscuits 21. Susie 22. Emma 23. Auntie 24. Empty caravan 25. Newspaper cutting 26. Garden door 27. Roadman's hut 28. Thorney-Copse Wood 29. Drawers 30. Scar 31. Rose 32. Exercising 33. Good repair.

CHAPTER TWELVE

How Very Annoying!

THAT'S QUEER. THERE REALLY ISN'T ANYWHERE FOR HER TO HIDE HERE. WHY DID SHE THROW HER CASE UP THESE STAIRS AND THEN RUSH AWAY? SHE MIGHT GUESS WE'D FIND IT. WHERE IS SHE? ELIZABETH!
WELL, I'M GOING TO OPEN THE CASE. I FEEL THERE'S SOMETHING PECULIAR ABOUT ALL THIS. I HOPE IT ISN'T LOCKED.
IT WASN'T. INSIDE WAS A CARDBOARD BOX, TIED WITH STRING...
GOSH– LOOK! IT'S GOT 'THE MONEY' PRINTED ON IT! OPEN IT UP, PETER.
THE MONEY
THE BOX WAS HURRIEDLY OPENED, ONLY TO REVEAL...
ANOTHER BOX!
PUZZLINGLY, THE SECOND BOX CONTAINED YET ANOTHER. BUT INSIDE THAT...
HELLO, WHAT'S THIS? A BLANK CARD...
PERHAPS THERE'S SOMETHING ON THE OTHER SIDE.
THERE WAS. BUT PETER COULD BARELY BELIEVE HIS EYES...
WHAT DOES IT SAY? WHAT DOES IT SAY?
IT SAYS 'LOTS AND LOTS OF LOVE FROM SUSIE!' OH! I'D LIKE TO SLAP HER! MAKING US CHASE AFTER HER– LEAVING THAT SILLY HANKY BY THE STILE — AND MAKING US UNDO ALL THOSE BOXES!
THE SECRET SEVEN WERE VERY, VERY ANGRY– ESPECIALLY JACK...
HOW DARE SHE PLAY A TRICK LIKE THAT! JUST WAIT TILL I GET HOME. I'LL HAVE SOMETHING TO SAY TO HER!

WHERE'S SHE GONE? I DIDN'T SEE HER AFTER WE TURNED THE CORNER. SHE MUST HAVE HAD HER BICYCLE HIDDEN SOMEWHERE HERE.
SHE PLANNED IT ALL VERY WELL. I MUST SAY SHE'S JOLLY CLEVER. GOSH— I REALLY DID THINK WE'D GOT HOLD OF ELIZABETH THAT TIME!
SUSIE MUST HAVE LAUGHED LIKE ANYTHING WHEN SHE PRINTED THE INITIALS E.M.W.S. ON THAT CHEAP OLD SUIT-CASE. I RECOGNISE IT NOW—IT'S BEEN UP IN OUR LOFT FOR AGES.
EMWS
WELL, COME ON—LET'S GET HOME. I'M TIRED OF TALKING ABOUT SUSIE.
AS THEY RODE AWAY, PETER BEGAN TO ARRANGE THE NIGHT'S MEETING AT BRAMBLE COTTAGE WITH GEORGE, JACK AND COLIN. THE GIRLS WERE SAD THAT THEY COULD NOT JOIN THEM...
YOU ALWAYS LEAVE US OUT OF THESE NIGHT ADVENTURES.
DON'T YOU DARE TO LET ANYTHING OUT TO SUSIE ABOUT TONIGHT. WE CAN'T HAVE HER RUINING EVERYTHING. I DO WONDER HOW ELIZABETH GETS INTO THE HOUSE. SHE MUST HAVE AN EXTRA KEY.
THERE MAY BE A POLICE-MAN OR TWO AS WELL. I VOTE WE GET THERE BEFORE THEY DO—OR THEY'LL GET RATHER A SHOCK WHEN THEY HEAR A WHOLE COLLECTION OF PEOPLE TAKING UP THEIR POSITIONS HERE AND THERE IN THE GARDEN!
THEY ARRANGED TO MEET AT TEN PAST TEN, AND CYCLE ALL TOGETHER TO BELLING...
WE'LL HIDE OUR BIKES UNDER THE NEARBY HEDGE AND GET INTO THE GARDEN AT THE BACK. REMEMBER TO HOOT IF THERE'S ANY DANGER.
THIS IS AWFULLY EXCITING. I ONLY HOPE SUSIE DOESN'T HEAR ME GETTING UP AND GOING DOWNSTAIRS.
JACK—IF YOU DO ANYTHING SILLY SO THAT SUSIE FOLLOWS YOU, I'LL DISMISS YOU FROM THE SECRET SEVEN!
AND PETER REALLY MEANT IT!

Puppy Care

Peter and Janet love to think back to the time when Scamper was a puppy, although *they* preferred to call him 'a little bundle of mischief'! They remember how excited they were when they went to the breeder to collect him, and what fun they had looking after him, playing with him and training him. Of course, Scamper's fully grown now, but Peter and Janet have written down the following tips for all those readers who have their own 'bundles of mischief'—or hope to have one soon.

Choosing your puppy

You'll be able to choose your puppy when it is about six weeks old. The breeder will tell you about the puppy's general health, but you can look for your own signs of fitness: a healthy puppy will be fat, have clear eyes and be mischievous. The occasional visit to see the puppy during the next two or three weeks will help to make sure it is continuing in good health.

Taking your puppy home

At eight or nine weeks the puppy will be ready to take home. Be sure to find out which inoculations the puppy has had (the breeder should give you a certificate bearing these details). An early visit to the vet will see that any other important vaccinations are given.

Remember that at first your puppy will be frightened and homesick in its new surroundings, so be gentle and quiet with it while it gets used to its new home.

A warm, comforting hot-water bottle (wrapped in an old pullover) will help it to settle down in its bed. For the first few nights you could keep the puppy in your room, where you can speak reassuringly to it when it whimpers, but be sure it has its own bed—perhaps a basket with an old blanket. A dog

needs somewhere of its own where it can chew bones, sleep and enjoy being alone. Don't disturb or waken a dog once it has taken to its bed.

Feeding

Puppies should be fed four times each day—two meals of meat and two of milk. Follow closely the diet sheet supplied by the breeder (if he doesn't give you one, obtain one from your vet) and be sure not to change the diet suddenly as this will upset the pup's tummy and cause it distress.

Calcium powder and cod-liver oil (dosage according to the manufacturer) should be added to one meal each day until the dog is fully grown. You may find the puppy will take it from a spoon.

Always have water available, and remember to change this daily.

House training

Begin by training your puppy on newspaper, preferably in a room without carpeting and from which

Continued on page 82

Home Printing is Easy!

"Susie must have laughed like anything when she printed the letters E.M.W.S. on that cheap old suitcase," said Jack—and he was right. Susie had great fun working out how to make printing blocks, choosing the right inks and then printing the letters, one by one, on the lid of the case. It kept her amused for a whole morning—and it was easy to do.

You could do some home printing. You could design and print identity cards and badges for your club. Or you could make your own pictures, greetings cards or wrapping paper. All you need are some printing blocks (below you can read how to make them), some water-based inks or powder paint, and non-shiny paper.

You can make a printing block from any firm vegetable, such as a potato, carrot, swede or parsnip. Cut the vegetable in half, and let it dry for a few minutes. Then, with a pencil, draw on one of the flat surfaces the outline of the letter or picture which you want to print. But remember that most letters need to be formed back to front on the blocks, otherwise the letters will print the wrong way round. Next, with an adult's help, cut away the part of the vegetable outside of the outline, so that you are left with the letter or picture. Cover the printing surface with paint or ink and press it down firmly on to the paper, then carefully lift the block so that you don't smudge the printing. By printing the design over and over again, and by using different colours, you can make all sorts of interesting patterns.

You could also . . .

Experiment with potatoes of various shapes, using their basic outline as part of your design. . . .

Try printing in white or light colours on dark paper. . . .

Carve silhouettes of your friends' faces in potatoes and print them to make personal birthday cards or wrapping paper. . . .

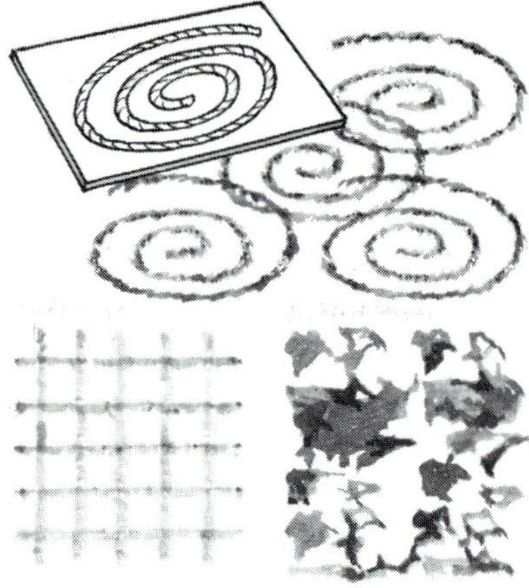

Print the design for your club badges on stiff white card. Cut them out in squares or circles, and fix safety-pins to the backs with adhesive tape.

Another method of making blocks is to use a small piece of wood or thick card (or even a ceramic tile), strong glue and some string. Cover the base of the wood or card with glue and arrange the string in a pattern on the glue. Leave it to dry before adding the ink and printing in the same way as with the vegetable blocks.

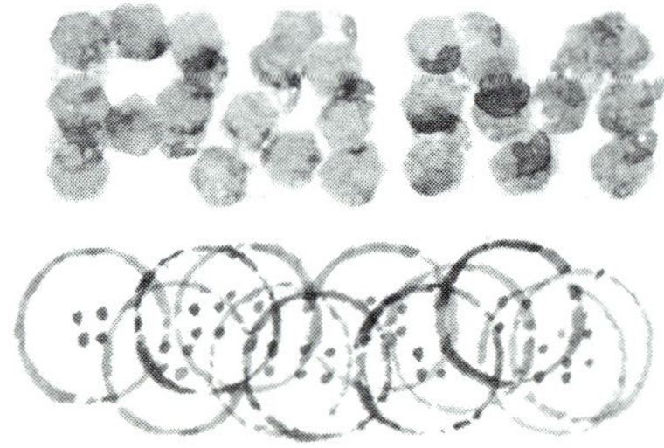

Instead of string you could use twigs, old matchsticks or even coins. Or you could print patterns directly from objects such as scraps of wood, shells, bottle caps or the end of a pencil. Or perhaps you'll have some ideas of your own—now you know that home printing is easy!

CHAPTER THIRTEEN

Waiting and Watching

The boys met together and cycled over to the grandmother's house in Belling

THAT night Peter, Jack, George and Colin slipped silently out of their houses. Jack was very much afraid that Susie might hear him, but when he put his ear to her door, he could hear gentle little snores. Good—she was asleep! He remembered Peter's threat to dismiss him from the Secret Seven if he wasn't careful about Susie, and he felt very glad to hear those snores!

The boys met together and then cycled quickly over to the grandmother's house in Belling. They met nobody at all, not even a policeman, and were very thankful.

The four of them dismounted quietly and put their bicycles into the hedge beyond Bramble Cottage. The cottage was in complete darkness.

"The only person to hoot is *me*,' whispered Peter. 'If we all hoot when we hear or see something interesting or suspicious, it would sound as if the garden was *full* of owls—and any policeman would be jolly suspicious!'

'All right,' whispered back George. 'Can we choose our own hiding-places? What about two of us going to hide in the garden at the front of the house, and two at the back?'

'No—two at the back, one in the front—you, Colin—and one at the side where the side-door is,' said Peter, in a low voice. 'Don't forget that Miss Wardle said she thought Elizabeth might have a key to that door—and there are no bolts there on the inside!'

'Oh, yes!' said Jack. 'I'll go and hide in the hedge beside the garden door, Peter. There isn't any door on the fourth side. We shall be watching every door there is—and every window.'

'It's very dark,' said Peter, looking up at the sky. 'There's no moon, and it's a cloudy night, so there are no stars either. We shall have to keep our ears wide open, because it may be pretty difficult to see anything.'

'Our eyes will soon get used to the darkness,' said Colin. 'I say—listen, what's that?' He clutched at Peter and made him jump.

A slight noise came from near by, and then a shadow loomed up. A voice spoke. 'It's me—Tom. I was waiting here, and I heard you. Where are you hiding?'

They told him. 'Well, I think *I'll* climb up a tree,' said Tom, in a low voice. 'That will be a very good place to watch from—or listen from! I don't think any policemen are about. I've been here for some time.'

'Hoot if you hear anyone coming,' Peter reminded him. 'I'll hoot back. But only you or I will hoot.'

'I'll find a tree to climb,' whispered Tom. 'See—that one over there, near the wall. I shall have a good view from there—if only the clouds clear and the stars shine out!'

The four went to find their own hiding-places, feeling pleasantly excited. This *was* fun! They heard Tom climbing his tree. Then there was silence. Peter was snuggled into a bush, from where he could keep good watch.

A sudden screech made everyone jump, and their hearts beat fast. Whatever was it? Then a white shadow swept round the dark garden, and everyone heaved a sigh of relief.

'Only a barn-owl!' thought Peter. 'Goodness—it made me jump. Good thing it doesn't hoot, only screeches—or we would all of us have thought that someone was coming!'

Nothing happened for a while—then a low, quavering hoot came across the garden. 'Hoo! Hoo-hoo-hoo-hoooooooo!'

'That's Tom!' thought Peter, and he and the others in hiding stiffened, and listened hard, trying to see

He could see the beam moving here and there behind the drawn curtains!

through the darkness.

Then someone brushed by Peter's bush and he crouched back in fright. He heard a little cough—a man's cough. It must be a policeman who had come along so quietly that no one but Tom had heard him. Peter waited a few seconds till he was sure that the man had found a hiding-place, and then he hooted too.

'Hoo! Hoo-hoo-hoo-hooooooo!'

Now everyone must guess that at least one policeman was in the garden! Peter's heart began to thump. Suddenly things seemed very strange and very exciting—all the dark shadows around, and so many people waiting! He half hoped that Elizabeth would not come to her granny's house that night. It would be so frightening for her to be surrounded suddenly by complete strangers!

Then suddenly he stared in amazement. Was that a *light* he saw in one of the upstairs rooms of the house? A light like that made by a torch? Yes—it was! He could see the beam moving here and there behind the drawn curtains!

Elizabeth must be there—she must have got in somehow, in spite of everyone watching! Or could it be Miss Wardle creeping about with a torch? No—surely she would switch on a light!

Peter gave a hoot again. 'Hoooo! Hoo-hoo-hoo-hoooooooooo!' That would make certain that everyone was on guard. If Elizabeth had got in, then she would have to get out—and surely one of them would see her!

The light in the upstairs room disappeared—and reappeared again in another room. Peter thought it was the kitchen. Perhaps the hungry runaway girl was looking for food again?

How HAD she got in? But, more important still—where was she going to come out?

All About Owls

'Only a barn owl!' thought Peter. 'Good thing it doesn't hoot, only screeches.' Good thing, too, that Peter recognised a barn owl when he heard one, and knew that different species of owls make different noises. Would *you* have known that if you had been one of the boys hiding in the garden of Bramble Cottage that evening?

There are five species of owls resident in this country—plus the snowy owl, which sometimes visits Scotland—and they all have their own individual characteristics.

The tawny owl is the one with the hoo-hoo-hoo-hoooooooo hoot that Peter was mimicking in the garden. It is the best known owl of all, although it usually stays in woodlands, and doesn't often venture near human habitation. By day it hides away in a quiet corner of the wood, hoping to avoid being discovered by the small woodland birds which will come and torment it. But at night the tawny owl emerges into the open, full of confidence, its eyes wide open and enormous, ready to pounce on the small mammals and birds on which it feeds.

If you do happen to see an owl by day, the chances are that it will be a little owl—a foreign species that was introduced into this country at the end of the last century. Although it is little more than half the size of other owls, it will attack birds larger than itself. Most little owls feed on animals and insects, however.

The owl least often seen is the long-eared owl, which hides itself away in dark, gloomy pine-woods. Much more common is the short-eared owl. (Actually, the 'ears' from which both these species take their name are not ears at all—they are simply tufts of feathers on their heads. Owls, like other birds, have their ears on the sides of their heads, concealed by feathers.)

Short-eared owls hunt by day as

well as by night in open, treeless countryside, choosing voles and mice as their main diet. And, unlike other owls that hoot or screech, short-eared owls squawk like a cat or bark.

Barn owls have many ways of expressing themselves besides screeching. They can hiss, snore, chirrup—and even purr when they're pleased with themselves. As their name suggests, they live in barns and other farm buildings, or ruins, as well as woods, and they usually remain hidden by day.

No owls are very enthusiastic nest-builders, but of them all the barn owl is quite the most untidy housekeeper. It doesn't bother to make itself a proper nest, and never clears up all the mess it makes around its home.

Owls are very responsible parents, though, and they won't hesitate to reprimand anyone who dares to interfere with their family. So beware of taking pity on any young owlet you may find that has tumbled out of its nest or wandered off and got lost. Unless the little bird is hurt and needs attention, resist the urge to touch it. Even though it's true that owls make delightful pets, once removed from the care of its parents an owlet will never learn to hunt or fend for itself.

CHAPTER FOURTEEN

A Real Mystery!

THE light from the torch inside the house moved here and there. Then it disappeared completely, as if it had been switched off. All the watchers listened, and strained their eyes in the darkness. Now Elizabeth would be leaving the house, and they must stop her. What door—or what window—would she creep from?

Nothing happened. No door opened. No window creaked or rattled. For ten whole minutes the watchers stood silent and tense. Then a man's voice called from somewhere in the garden.

'Will! Seen anyone?'

To Peter's intense surprise another man's voice answered. 'No. Not a thing. The kid must be still in the house. We'll knock up Miss Wardle and search.'

So there were *two* policemen in the garden then! How very quiet the other one had been! The boys were most surprised. *Now* what should they do? They watched the policemen switch on torches and heard them go to the front door of the house.

Peter hooted once more, and the others, realizing that he wanted them, left their hiding-places and came cautiously to find him. Tom slid down the tree and joined them too.

'The policemen didn't hear or see anyone—any more than we did!' said Peter. 'We could only have seen what they saw—a light in the downstairs of the house. Tom, did *you* see anything else?'

'Not a thing,' said Tom. 'Look—I'll slip off, I think. The police don't know me, and they might wonder what I'm doing here with you. So long!'

He disappeared into the night and left the four boys together. They went near to the front door, at which the policemen had rung a minute ago, keeping in the dark shadows. The door was being opened cautiously by a very scared Miss Wardle, dressed in a long green dressing-gown, her hair in pins.

'Oh—it's you!' the boys heard her say to the police. 'Come in. I'm afraid I was asleep, although I said I'd try and keep awake tonight. Do you want me to go and see if anything is taken?'

'Well, Miss Wardle, we know that *someone* was in your house just now,' said one of the policemen. 'We saw the light of a torch in two rooms. One of us would like to come in and search, please—the other will stay out here in case the girl—if it is the girl—tries to make a run for it. We haven't seen her come out—or go in either for that matter! But we did see the light of her torch.'

'Oh, I see. Well, come in, then,' said Miss Wardle. 'But please make no noise, or you'll scare the old lady. Come into the kitchen—I can soon tell if food is gone again.'

The policeman disappeared into the

'I can soon tell if food is gone again'

cottage with Miss Wardle, leaving the other man on guard in the garden. The four boys watched from the safety of the shadows. Surely Elizabeth must be in the house? She couldn't have left by any door or window without being seen or heard! They watched lights going on in each room, as Miss Wardle and the policeman searched.

After what seemed like a very long time, they heard voices in the hall. Miss Wardle came to the door with the policeman.

'Nothing to report, Will,' said the policeman to the man left on guard. 'Nobody's in the house. Miss Wardle even went into the old lady's room to make sure the girl hadn't crept in there, feeling that she was cornered.'

'Well—nobody's come *out* of the house,' said Will, sounding surprised. 'Has anything been taken?'

'Yes—more food. Nothing else,' said the first policeman. 'Queer, isn't it? How could anyone have got in under our very eyes and ears—taken food—and got out again without being heard or seen going away? Well—thanks, Miss Wardle. Sorry to have been such a nuisance for nothing. How that girl—and it *must* be the girl—gets in and out like this beats me. And where she's hiding beats me too. We've combed the countryside for her! Well—her brother's coming over to this country tomorrow—not that *he* can do much, if we can't!'

The police departed. The front door shut. The light went off in the hall, and then one appeared upstairs. Then that went out too. Miss Wardle was presumably safely in bed again.

'What do you make of it, Peter?' whispered Jack. 'Peculiar, isn't it?'

'Yes. I can't understand it,' said Peter. 'I mean—there were us four hiding here—and two policemen—and Tom up the tree—and yet not one of us saw Elizabeth getting in and out—and not one of us even *heard* her.'

'And yet she must have come here, into this garden,' said Jack. 'She broke in somewhere—or unlocked a door—she even put on her torch in the house to see what she could take—and then she got out again, with us all watching and listening—and disappeared. No—I don't understand it either.'

'Come on—let's go home and sleep on it,' said Peter. 'I feel tired now, with all the waiting and watching—and the excitement—and now the disappointment. Poor Elizabeth—what must she be feeling, having to scrounge food at night, and hide away in the daytime? She must be very miserable.'

'Well—maybe her brother can help,' said Colin. 'He'll be here tomorrow. Come on—I'm going home!'

'Come on—let's go home and sleep on it,' said Peter

Butterflies and Moths

The Secret Seven are so glad they live in the countryside—there's so much wild life to see! They particularly like the many types of butterflies and moths which they spot as they cycle around while trying to solve mysteries. Janet thought that butterflies and moths were themselves something of a mystery, so she decided to investigate them—and this is what she discovered . . .

All butterflies and moths belong to a 'family' of insects known as the Lepidoptera, a word which means 'scale wings'. The picture above right shows how these scales—thousands of them—overlap to form the butterfly's wings.

There is a greater variety of moths than butterflies, ranging from the giant owlet moth, which comes from South America and measures 30 cm from one wing-tip to the other, to tiny moths which measure only 3 mm across.

It is not easy to say exactly what is the difference between butterflies and moths, but, as a general rule, butterflies have club-like tips to their feelers, or antennae; moths, on the other hand, have various types of feelers, but rarely are they club-tipped.

All butterflies and moths go through the same changes during their lifetime, however. Each one begins as an egg, out of which comes a caterpillar, which develops into a winged insect. At first its wings are tiny and crumpled, so the first thing a moth or butterfly does is to climb up to some place where it can hang out its wings to dry. After only a few hours these are firm enough to support the insect in flight, and off it goes—perhaps into your garden!

Most moths and butterflies eat nectar and other sweet substances, so one of the best ways to encourage them to fly into your garden is to plant those flowers with plenty of nectar, like Aubrietia and Michaelmas daisies.

There are about 100,000 sorts of butterflies and moths, so if you want to make the study of Lepidoptera your hobby, now's a good time to start because it would take a lifetime to spot all the different species!

Silver Barred Charaxes

Monarch

Brimstone

Adonis Blue

CHAPTER FIFTEEN

Crosspatches

THE four boys belonging to the Secret Seven overslept the next morning. They were so tired from their long watch the night before! Janet was cross when Peter wouldn't wake, because she was longing to know what happened!

'Gosh—I'll be terribly late for school,' groaned Peter, leaping out of bed. 'You might have waked me before, Janet.'

'Well, I squeezed a sponge of cold water over you, and yelled in your ear, and pulled all the clothes off!' said Janet indignantly. 'And Scamper barked his head off. What *more* would you like me to do? And what happened last night?'

'Nothing. Absolutely nothing!' said Peter, dressing hurriedly. 'I mean, we didn't get Elizabeth—she got into the house, took what she wanted, and got out again—and disappeared. And although there were seven people altogether in the garden, watching, nobody saw her. So you see—nothing happened. ALL RIGHT, MOTHER! I'M JUST COMING.'

He tore downstairs with his mother still calling him, ate his breakfast standing up, and then cycled to school at top speed. He yelled to Janet as he left her at the corner.

'Meeting tonight at five-thirty. Tell Pam and Barbara!'

The meeting was not very thrilling. After such high hopes of something

He tore downstairs and ate his breakfast standing up

really exciting happening the night before, everyone felt flat. Pam made them all cross by saying that if *she* had hidden in the garden she would certainly have heard or seen Elizabeth creeping by.

'You must have fallen asleep,' she said. 'You really must. I mean—*seven* of you there! And nobody heard a thing! I bet you fell asleep.'

'Be quiet,' said Peter crossly. 'You don't know what you're talking about, Pam. Now don't start again. BE QUIET, I say!'

'Well,' said Pam, obstinately, 'all I can say is that if Elizabeth *really* didn't get in or out, and it seems like that to me, or you'd have heard her—then she must be hiding in some jolly good place *inside* the house.'

'The police searched all over it,' said Peter. 'I did think of that bright idea myself—but I gave it up when the policeman hunted all through the cottage last night without finding Elizabeth. After all, it's only a small place—no cellars—no attics. We did hear *one* thing of interest, though. The brother who's in France is arriving in this country today. Maybe he'll have something to say that will be of help.'

'Well—why don't you go and see him, then?' said Pam, who was in a very persistent mood that day. 'You could tell him what *you* know—about Tom the stable-boy seeing Elizabeth in Gorton, for instance.'

'H'm. That's the first sensible remark you've made, Pam,' said Peter. He turned to Jack. 'Will you come with me, Jack? I'd like to see the brother, I must say.'

'Wuff-wuff-wuff!' said Scamper, suddenly.

'*Now* what's the matter?' said Peter, whose late night had made him decidedly impatient that day. 'What's Scamper barking for? If it's Susie I'll have a few sharp words to say to her about playing that fat-headed trick on us with the suit-case!'

It *was* Susie. She stood grinning at the door when Peter opened it. 'Mint sauce!' she said promptly. 'Let me in. I've some clues—great big ones. I know where Elizabeth is and what she's doing. I . . .'

'You do NOT!' yelled a furious Peter, and called for Jack. 'Jack—pull her by

Susie found herself being dragged to the gate

the hair all the way home. Pam, Barbara, Janet—get hold of her frock and pull too. Come on! Get going!'

And for once in a way the cheeky Susie was taken by surprise and found herself being dragged to the gate, and not very gently either!

'All right!' she yelled, kicking and hitting out as vigorously as she could. 'I shan't tell you my big clues. But you'll see I'm right! And I know your password, see! Mint sauce, mint sauce, mint sauce!'

She disappeared up the lane, and the Seven went back to the shed, feeling better for the excitement.

'Now we shall have to alter our password,' said Peter, in disgust. 'How did Susie know it, Jack? Have you been saying it in your sleep, or something?'

'No,' said Jack, still angry. 'She must have hidden somewhere near the shed and heard us saying it. Blow Susie! You don't think she really *does* know something, do you?'

'How can she?' said Peter. 'And why can't you keep her in order? If Janet behaved like that I'd spank her.'

'You would *not*,' said Janet, indignantly. 'You just try it!'

'Gosh—we really are crosspatches today!' said Barbara, surprised. 'The boys must be tired after their late night! Well—have we any plans?'

'Only that Jack and I will go and see Elizabeth's brother, if he's arrived at the grandmother's,' said Peter, calming down. 'He'll be sure to go there, because his sister is known to be somewhere near. Come on, Jack—I'm fed up with this meeting. Let's go!'

How do You Rate?

Would *you* make a good Secret Seven member? If you're sharp-eyed, quick-witted and have 'staying power', probably you would, for these are the three most important factors which each member of the Seven possesses. Below are some simple tests designed to assess your abilities. See how well you can do, remembering that each member of the Seven passed these tests with flying colours! Check your answers with those on page 82.

SEEING DOUBLE
The six pictures below look identical at first glance, but only two are *exactly* the same. Can you spot them? (Score 10 points for correct answer.)

NAME GAME
As you can see, in the test below there is one letter for each of the vacant boxes. But the letters are not in the correct positions. Can you fit them into the spaces so that the letters inside the boxes spell out the name (Christian and surname) of one of the characters in the story? (Score 10 points for correct answer.)

	H		R		E		S		N		I		G

N O N C L S A

MISSING NUMBER
Can you work out what the missing number is? (Score 10 points for correct answer.)

12	7	6

12	3	

12	5	8

MEMORY TEST
When Peter and Janet were clearing out their cupboard in the search for things to give Mrs Sonning for the jumble sale, they came across all sorts of old toys and playthings. Some of them are shown below. To test your memory, study these items for 15 seconds, then turn the book over and write down, within 60 seconds, all the items you can remember. There are 14 altogether. (Score 14 points if you can remember all the items.) When you've done this, write down the first letter of each item and re-arrange these letters to form the name of some things (two words, 6, 8) which were eaten and enjoyed at some time during the story. (Score 6 points if you find the correct food.)

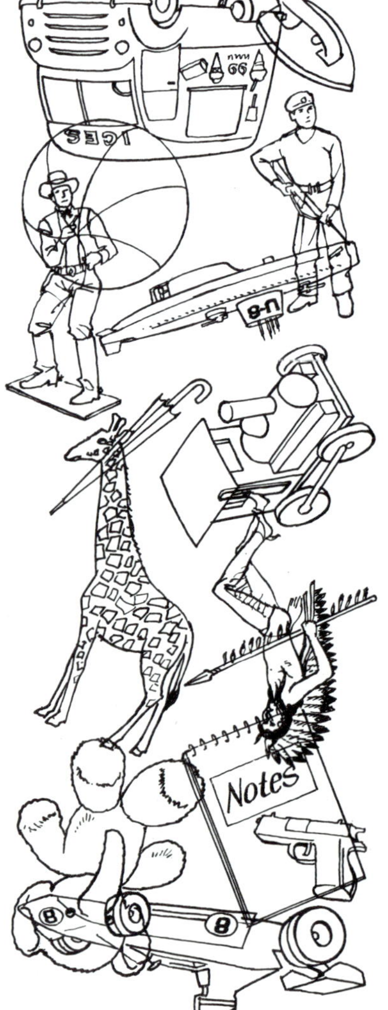

CHAPTER SIXTEEN

Unexpected News

PETER and Jack arrived at Bramble Cottage on their bicycles, and at once heard voices there. They put their cycles by the gate and looked over the hedge.

Three people were sitting in deck-chairs in the little garden, enjoying the warm evening sunshine. One was Miss Wardle—one was an old lady, obviously the grandmother—and one was a youth of about eighteen, looking very worried.

'He must be the brother,' said Peter. 'Good, he's arrived! Come on. We'll go up the front path, and if Miss Wardle sees us, she'll call us and we'll go over and talk.'

Miss Wardle did see them, and recognized them at once. 'Oh,' she said to the old lady beside her, 'those are the two nice boys who brought all that jumble. Come here, boys—I'm sure Mrs Sonning would like to thank you.'

Peter and Jack walked over. 'Good evening,' said Peter, politely. 'I do hope you have news of your grand-daughter, Mrs Sonning.'

'No. We haven't,' said the old lady, and to Peter's alarm, a tear rolled down her cheek. 'This is my grandson, Charles, her brother. He's come over from France to see if he can help, because Elizabeth is very fond of him. If she knows he is here, she may come out of hiding.'

'We met a boy the other day who saw her in Gorton,' said Peter. 'She must

'Those are the two nice boys who brought all that jumble. Come here, boys—I'm sure Mrs Sonning would like to thank you'

'One of the stable-boys up at Warner's Stables there,' said Peter, pointing up the hill

have been on her way here then.'

'What!' said the boy Charles. 'Someone actually saw her in *Gorton*! But that's *not* on the way here. Who was this boy?'

'One of the stable-boys up at Warner's Stables there,' said Peter, pointing up the hill. 'He said Elizabeth told him she was going to France to see you.'

'But she didn't know where I *was* in France,' said Charles. 'I've been travelling around all the time! Even the police only got in touch with me with great difficulty! I'm certain that Elizabeth wouldn't have been mad enough to try to find me when she didn't even know what part of France I was in!'

'Well,' said Peter, 'that's what *Tom* said she told him, and he couldn't very well have made it up, because he had never met her before!'

'I'll go and see him,' said Charles, and got up—but just then the telephone bell shrilled out, the noise coming clearly into the garden.

'Answer it, Charles, there's a dear,' said old Mrs Sonning, and the boy went indoors. Peter and Jack waited patiently for him, and were immensely surprised to see him come running out again at top speed, his eyes shining and his face aglow.

'Granny! It was Elizabeth's headmistress. She . . .'

'Oh—has the child gone back to school—or gone back to her aunt?' said the old lady.

'No! But all that upset about the stolen money is cleared up!' said Charles, taking his grandmother's hand. 'It *wasn't* Elizabeth who took it, of course. The girl who stole it got frightened when the papers kept reporting that Elizabeth hadn't been found, and she suddenly owned up.'

'Who *was* the girl?' said Miss Wardle, indignantly.

'I'm afraid it was the one supposed to be Elizabeth's best friend,' said Charles. 'Lucy Howell—she came here to stay with Elizabeth last year, Granny. She saw the cash-box in the desk and took it on the spur of the moment, without even opening it. She hid it somewhere, waiting for a chance to break it open. She didn't realize that there was about twenty pounds in it, and she was horrified when the police were called in about it.'

'I should think so!' said Mrs Sonning. 'I never did like Lucy—a sly little thing I thought she was. I was sorry that she was Elizabeth's friend.'

'Well, apparently Lucy was annoyed with Elizabeth and very jealous of her just then, because Elizabeth was ahead of her in marks and doing better at games—and what did she do but take the cash-box and put it into Elizabeth's chest of drawers! When the boarders' trunks and chests were searched —Elizabeth is a weekly boarder as you know—the cash-box was found—still unopened! Elizabeth had gone home for the week-end to Aunt Rose's, and the police went there to question her.'

'Poor Elizabeth!' said Mrs Sonning. 'But didn't she deny taking the money?'

'Yes, of course—but she wasn't believed. Most unfortunately she had actually been in the form-room where the money had stupidly been left, doing some homework all by herself, and had been seen there. Aunt Rose was very upset—and poor Elizabeth felt there was nothing to do but run away! I expect she thought she might have to go to prison or something!'

'Poor child! But now she can come back with her name cleared!' said Mrs Sonning. 'What a dreadful thing to happen to someone like Elizabeth. She's as straight as can be.'

'Yes. But how are we going to let her know that everything is all right?' asked Miss Wardle. 'We don't even know where the child is!'

'No. That's true,' said Charles, worried. 'But we *must* find her! She took only enough money with her to pay her railway fare down here apparently—that's all she had. She wouldn't have enough to buy food or anything else. She's hiding somewhere, all alone, worried and miserable—thinking that we're all ashamed of her!'

'Don't,' said old Mrs Sonning, and began to weep into her handkerchief. 'Such a dear, good child—always so kind. Charles, we must find her—we must!'

'Well—the first thing to do is for me to go up and see this stable-boy who met Elizabeth in Gorton,' said Charles, getting up. 'Will you take me up to him, you two boys?'

'Yes,' said Peter and Jack, who had been listening to the conversation with much interest. 'We'll take you now. I say—we are glad everything's cleared up!'

Continued from page 63

there is access to a garden or other open space. Each time the pup has fed or woken from sleep, place it on the newspaper. It will soon realise you are waiting for it to relieve itself. When it has done this, praise it.

Change the paper, leaving a little of the soiled sheet in place so that the odour will remind the pup why the paper is there. If it wets in other places, scold it and take it to the paper. Praise it each time it uses the paper.

Move the paper slightly nearer the door each day, finally placing a sheet outside. The pup will quickly learn that it must wait by the door when it needs to relieve itself, and probably it will let you know by barking or tapping the door with its paw.

DOs and DON'Ts

Do be sure to pick up your puppy properly: place one hand under its

rump and the other under its chest, just behind its shoulders. Lift both hands together.

Don't overdo the brushing of your puppy. It needs to get used to this, but two or three minutes each day is enough to start with.

Do play with your puppy, but don't be rough, and don't force it to play if it's not in the mood. If it growls, reprimand it.

Don't forget that a puppy loves chewing, so to save your furniture provide the puppy with some tough leather or hard-rubber toys. All puppies love to chew beef-marrow bones, but never give a puppy bones that will splinter, or wooden or soft-rubber toys.

Do discipline your puppy—but neither bully nor pamper it. With the right balance you will produce a happy, contented pet which will become a close and faithful friend.

How Did You Do?

SECRET MESSAGE (page 15)

> ***We hope you enjoyed this tale about one of our adventures. Now we are looking for another puzzle to solve. Please tell us if you hear of one. But be careful not to let Susie know.***

TOWN JUMBLE (page 45)

The 20 towns and cities are: Blackpool, Portsmouth, Bristol, Coventry, London, Birmingham, Exeter, Reading, Newcastle, Glasgow, Edinburgh, Manchester, Scarborough, Swansea, Brighton, Bradford, Liverpool, Bournemouth, Lincoln, Windsor.

TRUE OR FALSE? (page 45)

1. False: breakfast. 2. True. 3. False: Bramble Cottage, Blackberry Lane. 4. True. 5. True. 6. False: Jack. 7. False: Monday. 8. False: top of steps. 9. True. 10. False: France.

THE HUNT IS ON (page 53)

> ***Bramble Cottage is a pretty little house in*** Belling ***Village. It is the home of Elizabeth's grandmother,*** Mrs Sonning, ***and her companion,*** Miss Wardle. ***When Peter and*** Jack ***first called there with some jumble for the*** Belling Women's Institute ***sale, they· learnt that some*** tarts, ***biscuits and a*** meat pie ***had disappeared from the kitchen the night before. More food had gone by the time the boys returned to the cottage*** two ***days later. So Peter and*** Jack ***decided that they would keep watch on Bramble Cottage*** that night.

SCORE RATINGS

Maximum score of 80 points

70-80 Excellent: you would make a good Secret Seven member.

60-70 Good: you have the potential; work just a little harder.

30-60 Fair: there's plenty of room for improvement, although you *could* qualify; more effort is needed.

SEEING DOUBLE (page 78)

2 and 6 are identical.

NAME GAME (page 78)

Charles Sonning.

MISSING NUMBER

The missing number is 10. Subtract the middle number from the number on the left, then add one to obtain the number on the right.

MEMORY TEST

Ginger biscuits. (Gun, Indian, notebook, giraffe, elephant, racing-car, ball, iron, soldier, cowboy, umbrella, ice-cream van, train, submarine.)

CHAPTER SEVENTEEN

A Funny Business Altogether

'Hey, Tom!' called Peter. 'There's someone wants to see you'

PETER, Jack, and Charles went up the hill to Warner's Stables, the two boys wheeling their bicycles. They liked Charles. He reminded them of someone, but they couldn't think who it was.

'Where's Tom?' Peter called to Harry, when they came to the stables.

'Somewhere about,' he shouted back. 'Over there, I think.'

'You see if Tom is over yonder, and I'll go into the stables and see if he's there,' said Peter. Charles went with Jack, and Peter looked into the stables. At the far end he saw Tom, cleaning out one of the stalls.

'Hey, Tom!' called Peter. 'There's someone wants to see you.'

'Who?' shouted back Tom.

'You remember meeting that girl Elizabeth?' said Peter. 'Well, it's her brother, Charles. He's come over from France, he's so upset, and . . .'

He stopped, because Tom had suddenly flung down his fork, and had shot past him at top speed. He tore out of the door, and Peter stared in surprise. When Peter got to the stable door himself, there was no sign of Tom! He saw Jack and Charles coming towards him.

'Did you see Tom? He tore out of here just now, goodness knows why!'

'We saw someone racing off,' said Jack. 'Blow! Just as we wanted him. Didn't you tell him someone wanted to see him?'

'Yes, of course. I don't know if he heard me or not, but he suddenly flung down his fork and dashed off without a word!' said Peter, puzzled.

Harry, the other stable-boy, came up with the big stable-girl. 'Don't take any notice of Tom,' he said. 'He's a bit queer! Isn't he, Kate?'

The stable-girl nodded. 'Hasn't got much to say for himself,' she said. 'Funny boy—a bit potty, *I* think!'

'But where did he go?' said Peter. 'Do you know where he lives? We could go to his home, and then our friend here could ask him a few things he wants to know.'

Neither Harry nor the girl knew where Tom lived, so Jack and Peter gave it up. 'Sorry,' they said to Charles and

Harry came up with the big stable-girl

Peter added: 'We could come here again tomorrow, if you like. Not that Tom can really tell you anything of importance. He may even have made it all up about meeting Elizabeth. He may have read about her in the papers, and just invented the whole meeting! He really *is* a bit queer, I think.'

'Well—thank you,' said Charles, who looked worried again. 'I'll go back. My poor old granny won't be herself again till we find Elizabeth. My parents haven't been told yet, but they'll have to be cabled tomorrow, and asked to come home. Dad's out in China on a most important job, and we didn't want to worry him at first. Apparently the police thought they would soon find my sister.'

'Yes—with no money—and wearing her school clothes it *ought* to have been easy to spot her,' said Jack. 'Well—goodbye—and good luck!'

The boys rode off down the hill. 'I'm jolly glad Elizabeth didn't steal that money after all,' said Peter. 'Though we've never met her, I thought it was rather queer that anyone said to be so honest and straightforward should have done such a thing. And now I've seen that old granny, and her nice brother Charles—he *is* nice, isn't he, Jack?—I see even more clearly that Elizabeth couldn't have been a thief.'

'It's a funny business altogether,' said Jack. 'And it's not cleared up yet, Peter—not till Elizabeth's found. Remember, *she* doesn't know that the real thief has owned up!'

'I know,' said Peter. 'Well—we'll have another Secret Seven meeting tomorrow night, the same time as today, Jack. We'll tell the others at school tomorrow. We'll have to report this evening's happenings, and see if there's anything further we can do.'

'Right!' said Jack. 'See you tomorrow!' and with a jingling of bicycle bells the two parted, each thinking the same thing. 'What a pity Elizabeth doesn't know that her name is cleared!'

Next evening the Secret Seven gathered in the meeting shed as usual, anxious to hear what Jack and Peter had to say. They were all very thrilled to hear about the brother Charles—and the exciting telephone call that had come while Jack and Peter were there.

'What a pity that boy Tom didn't stop and speak to Charles,' said Colin, puzzled. 'Do you suppose he made up that tale about meeting Elizabeth, and was afraid of being found out in his fairy-tale by Charles?'

'*I* tell you what!' said George, suddenly. 'I believe he knows where Elizabeth is! That's why he ran off like that—to warn her that her brother was there!'

'You may be right, George,' said Peter, considering the matter. 'Yes—perhaps he *does* know where she is! Well—all the more reason why we should go up tomorrow and see him! We'll ask him straight out if he knows where the girl is—and watch his face. He's sure to give himself away if he *does* know where she is—even if he swears he doesn't!'

'We'll tell Charles to come too,' said Jack. 'If *he* thinks Tom knows his sister's hiding-place, I've no doubt he'll be able to make him tell it!'

'Right,' said Peter. 'Well—tomorrow may be exciting. We'll just see!'

CHAPTER EIGHTEEN

Peter Goes Mad

AS THEY ARRIVED AT THE ENTRANCE TO THE MEADOW, PETER CALLED OUT—AND TOM CAME CANTERING OVER...
SORRY, I'M BUSY. IS THERE ANYTHING YOU WANT?
YES! TOM—I WANT TO ASK YOU A QUESTION. DO YOU KNOW WHERE ELIZABETH SONNING IS HIDING? DO YOU?
A FRIGHTENED LOOK CAME INTO TOM'S FACE...
WHY SHOULD I KNOW THAT? DON'T BE CRAZY!
WITHOUT ANOTHER WORD, TOM KICKED HIS HEELS AGAINST THE PONY'S SIDE AND GALLOPED OFF!
HE DOES KNOW! HE DOES AND HE WON'T TELL!
WHY, PETER—WHAT ON EARTH'S THE MATTER? WHY ARE YOU LOOKING LIKE THAT?
GOSH—OF COURSE HE KNOWS WHERE ELIZABETH IS! NOBODY IN THE WORLD KNOWS BETTER WHERE ELIZABETH HIDES OUT! NOBODY!
PETER! WHAT IS IT?
PETER!
HAVE YOU GONE MAD?
WHAT IN THE WORLD ARE YOU TALKING ABOUT? WHAT ARE YOU DOING?

BUT PETER DIDN'T ANSWER—HE JUST TOOK OFF AFTER TOM!
MAD! HE'S GONE ABSOLUTELY MAD!
COME HERE, YOU FATHEAD! EVERYTHING'S ALL RIGHT! ELIZABETH! COME HERE, I SAY! I'VE GOT GOOD NEWS FOR YOU! ELIZABETH! ELIZABETH!
EVERYTHING'S ALL RIGHT, I TELL YOU! LUCY HOWELL CONFESSED SHE TOOK THE MONEY! EVERYONE KNOWS IT WASN'T YOU! WILL YOU STOP, YOU ASS, AND LISTEN TO ME?
AT LAST THE PONY WAS BROUGHT TO A HALT...
COME ON! PERHAPS PETER HASN'T GONE MAD AFTER ALL. WHATEVER HE WAS SHOUTING ABOUT HAS MADE TOM STOP! HURRY!
YOU'RE ELIZABETH! I KNOW YOU ARE! I KNEW YOUR BROTHER REMINDED ME OF SOMEONE—AND I SUDDENLY SAW THE LIKENESS JUST NOW AT THE GATE! ELIZABETH, IT'S ALL RIGHT. YOUR NAME'S CLEARED. COME NOW, YOU ARE ELIZABETH, AREN'T YOU?
YES—I AM ELIZABETH SONNING! OH, IS IT TRUE THAT LUCY SAID SHE TOOK THE MONEY? I THOUGHT SHE HAD—BUT I WASN'T SURE. NOBODY WILL THINK ME A THIEF ANY MORE?
NOBODY. MY WORD, YOU'RE A PLUCKY KID, AREN'T YOU—GETTING A JOB AS A STABLE-BOY, AND WORKING HARD LIKE THIS! WHERE DID YOU HIDE AT NIGHT? HOW...?
OH—THERE'S CHARLES!
CHARLES! CHARLES! OH, I'M SO GLAD TO SEE YOU!

OH, CHARLES!
COME ON! ISN'T THIS GREAT!
YES, BUT WHAT A SURPRISING ENDING TO THE PROBLEM WE'VE BEEN PUZZLING OVER SO LONG!
WELL, YOU MONKEY! WHAT HAVE YOU GOT TO SAY FOR YOURSELF? BRINGING ME OVER FROM FRANCE LIKE THIS—HAVING EVERYONE HUNTING FOR YOU? WHERE HAVE YOU BEEN HIDING? HOW DID YOU GET IN AND OUT OF GRANNY'S HOUSE? WHY...?
OH, CHARLES—I'LL ANSWER ALL YOUR QUESTIONS! BUT LET'S GO TO GRANNY'S, DO LET'S. I DO WANT TO HUG HER, I DO WANT TO TELL HER EVERYTHING'S ALL RIGHT!
COME ON, THEN...
YOU KIDS CAN COME TOO. WE'VE A LOT TO THANK YOU FOR.
AND I'M LONGING TO KNOW HOW YOU SPOTTED THAT THIS DIRTY, UNTIDY, SMELLY STABLE-BOY WAS NO OTHER THAN MY NAUGHTY LITTLE SISTER ELIZABETH!

CHAPTER NINETEEN

A Jolly Good Finish

THEY all went out of the field, and took the path that led down to Bramble Cottage. The Seven were very thrilled to be in at the finish. To their great disgust they met Susie on her bicycle, riding along with a friend.

'Hallo!' she called cheekily. 'Solved your silly mystery yet?'

'Yes!' said Jack. 'And that boy Tom was Elizabeth—dressed up like a stable-boy! *You'd* never have thought of that in a hundred years!'

'Oh, but I knew it!' said the aggravating Susie. 'Shan't tell you how! But I knew it!' And away she went, waving her cheeky hand at them.

'She's a terrible fibber,' said Janet. 'I suppose she *couldn't* have guessed, could she, Jack?'

'I wouldn't put it past her,' said Jack, with a groan. 'Anyway, she'll keep on and on saying she knew. *Why* did I tell her just now?'

'Goodness knows,' said Peter. 'You'd better safety-pin your mouth, Jack! Well—here we are at the cottage. Won't the old granny be pleased!'

She was! She hugged the brown-faced, short-haired girl and kissed her and fondled her, happy tears streaming down her face.

Miss Wardle rushed indoors and brought out biscuits and lemonade for everyone. Scamper who was there as usual, of course, was delighted to have two fine biscuits presented to him.

'Elizabeth! Now where did you hide? And are those *my* riding-breeches?' asked Charles, pulling at them. 'Where did you get them?'

'From your chest of drawers here,' said Elizabeth. 'I knew nobody would miss them. They're rather big for me, though. And I've made them very dirty! I hid in the hayloft at the stables each

Miss Wardle brought out biscuits and lemonade for everyone

night, with just a rug to cover me. I was quite warm and cosy.'

'So you *did* take that rug!' said Miss Wardle. 'I thought so! And all that food too, I suppose?'

'Yes. You see, I'd no money left after paying my fare down here,' said Elizabeth. 'At least, I had five pence, that's all. So I had to get a job—but you're only paid once a week, so I had to have food till my wages were due—I couldn't go without eating!'

'You poor child!' said Miss Wardle. 'Bless you, I knew you were innocent, I knew you weren't a thief! Yes, and I cooked special tarts and pies for you, my little dear, and left them out, hoping you'd come and take them.'

'Oh—thank you!' said Elizabeth. 'I did wonder why there was such a *lot* of food in the larder—and food I especially liked!'

'Why did you tell us that you had met—well, met *yourself* in Gorton, and all that?' asked Peter, puzzled.

'Only to put you off the scent,' said Elizabeth. 'I thought if people imagined I was off to France to find Charles, they wouldn't guess I was hiding near Granny's. I had to come near Granny's because of getting food, you see—and, anyway, I wanted to *feel* I was near somebody belonging to me, I was so miserable.'

'How did you get into the house, Elizabeth?' said Miss Wardle, and Charles chimed in with:

'Yes—how did you?'

And Peter added, 'Why, the other night we all watched here in the garden—but, how very funny, you were here too, Elizabeth, pretending to watch for yourself—you were Tom, up that tree! *Were* you up the tree?'

Elizabeth laughed. 'Yes, of course. That tree has a branch that goes to the bathroom window—and I know how to open the window from the outside and slip in—I'll show you, it's quite easy if you have a pocket-knife. But I'm getting too large to squeeze through it now, really! It really made me laugh to think of everyone watching and waiting—and there was I, up the tree, waiting to slip through the window. I got a lovely lot of food that night—did you see my torch shining in the downstairs rooms? And I was just sliding down the tree again when I heard the police knocking on the front door.'

'And you told us not to tell the police you were there—because you knew your pockets were full of food!' said Peter, with a chuckle. 'Yes, I think your brother's right. You really are a monkey.'

'But I was a very, very good stable-boy,' said Elizabeth, earnestly. 'Granny, Mr Warner said he was very pleased with me, and he even promised me a rise in wages if I went on working so hard! Can I go on being a stable-boy? It's nicer than being at school.'

'Certainly not!' said her grandmother, smiling. 'You'll go back to school and be welcomed there by everyone—and you'll work hard and be top of the exams, although you've missed a week and a half!'

'But what *I* want to know is—how did *you*, Peter, realize that Tom the stable-boy was Elizabeth?' asked Charles.

'Well—I suddenly saw the likeness between you,' said Peter. 'And then somehow the bits of the jigsaw all fell into place, if you know what I mean! And I was so afraid that Elizabeth would run off again when she saw you, as she did when she heard you were at the stables yesterday, that I just felt I had to cycle at top speed after her pony and yell at her!'

'I was never so surprised in my life as when you came at me and my pony at sixty miles an hour on your bike, yelling at the top of your voice,' said Elizabeth. 'But I'm glad you did. Granny, I'm coming here for the holidays, aren't I? Can I have these children to play sometimes?'

'Of course!' said her grandmother. 'I shall always be glad to see them. There's only one thing I'm sad about, Elizabeth—your hair! *What* a pity you hacked it short like that. It was so soft and pretty!'

'I had to, Granny,' said Elizabeth. 'I did it with your nail scissors when I came one night to take Charles' riding-breeches to wear—and I took his jersey too, though it's so dirty now I don't expect he recognizes it! Oh, Granny—I'm so very happy. You can't think how different I feel!'

'We'd better go,' said Peter to the others, in a low voice. 'Let's leave them all to be happy together. Come on, say good-bye.'

They said good-bye, and Scamper gravely shook paws as well. Then away they went on their bicycles, Scamper running beside them.

'What a jolly fine finish!' said Jack. 'Who would have thought it would end like that? I feel rather happy myself! When's the next meeting, Peter?'

'Tomorrow—and we'll have a celebration to mark our success!' said Peter. 'Everyone must bring some food or drink. And we'll have to think of a new password, of course. What shall it be?'

'Stable-boy!' said Jack at once.

Well, it's quite a good one—but I mustn't tell you if it's the *right* one. Knock on the door of the shed, say 'Stable-boy!' and see if the Secret Seven let you in!

'Let's leave them all to be happy together'